W9-CJC-874

# CREATION
*of the*
# MODERN MIDDLE EAST

# Saudi Arabia

# CREATION

*of the*

# MODERN MIDDLE EAST

Iran, Second Edition

Iraq, Second Edition

Israel, Second Edition

Jordan, Second Edition

Lebanon

The Palestinian National Authority,
Second Edition

Saudi Arabia, Second Edition

Syria, Second Edition

Turkey, Second Edition

United Arab Emirates

# CREATION
## *of the*
## MODERN MIDDLE EAST

# Saudi Arabia

## Second Edition

Heather Lehr Wagner | Series Editor: Arthur Goldschmidt Jr.

CHELSEA HOUSE
PUBLISHERS
An imprint of Infobase Publishing

Chelsea House
An imprint of Infobase Publishing
132 West 31st Street
New York NY 10001

**Library of Congress Cataloging-in-Publication Data**
Wagner, Heather Lehr.
 Saudi Arabia / by Heather Lehr Wagner. — 2nd ed.
   p. cm. — (Creation of the modern Middle East)
 Includes bibliographical references and index.
 ISBN 978-1-60413-023-2 (hardcover)
 1. Saudi Arabia—Juvenile literature. I. Title. II. Series.
 DS204.25.W34 2008
 953.8—dc22    2008016912

Chelsea House books are available at special discounts when purchased in bulk quantities for businesses, associations, institutions, or sales promotions. Please call our Special Sales Department in New York at (212) 967-8800 or (800) 322-8755.

You can find Chelsea House on the World Wide Web at
http://www.chelseahouse.com

Series design by Annie O'Donnell
Cover design by Jooyoung An

Printed in the United States of America

Bang EJB 10 9 8 7 6 5 4 3 2 1

This book is printed on acid-free paper.

All links and Web addresses were checked and verified to be correct at the time of publication. Because of the dynamic nature of the Web, some addresses and links may have changed since publication and may no longer be valid.

# Contents

1    Trouble in the Kingdom     7

2    Shaping a Legend     16

3    The House of Saud     26

4    King of Arabia     40

5    Birth of a Nation     54

6    Death of a Nation Builder     68

7    The Diligent King     78

8    A Storm in the Desert     90

    Chronology and Timeline     100

    Bibliography     103

    Further Resources     105

    Picture Credits     106

    Index     107

    About the Contributors     112

# Trouble in the Kingdom

In the second half of the twentieth century, most Americans viewed Saudi Arabia as a strategic partner, a friendly nation in the turbulent Middle East, and—perhaps most important—a key supplier of oil. Most Americans were not really interested in the monarchy who ruled Saudi Arabia, the status of its citizens, or the fundamentalist Wahhabi branch of Islam practiced by many of its people.

All that changed on September 11, 2001. On that date, 19 members of the terrorist group al Qaeda launched a major attack against the United States. Fifteen of the nineteen terrorists were Saudi nationals. The 19 terrorists, in groups of four or five, boarded four planes at U.S. airports. The first group of five boarded American Airlines Flight 11 in Boston, a flight bound for Los Angeles. Within 30 minutes they had seized control of the plane. It crashed into the North Tower of the World Trade Center in New York City at 8:46 A.M.

The second group of terrorists also left from Boston, little more than 10 minutes after the first group. They were on board United Airlines Flight 175, heading for Los Angeles. Within 30 minutes the terrorists took control of the plane and headed for New York City, where the plane crashed into the South Tower of the World Trade Center at 9:03 A.M.

A third group of terrorists—the only group with four, rather than five, hijackers—boarded United Airlines Flight 93 and took off from Newark, New Jersey, at 8:42 A.M., bound for San

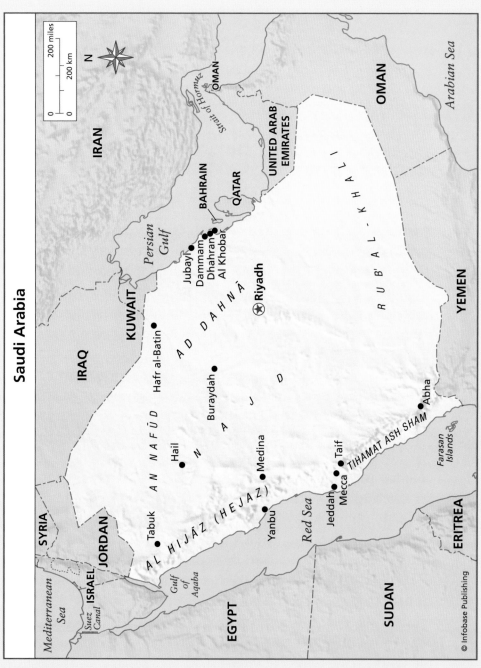

Saudi Arabia

Saudi Arabia, the largest country in the Middle East, is about one-fifth the size of the United States, and is home to about 27 million people. Although there are some mountains in the southwestern region of the country, Saudi Arabia is mostly desert and experiences extremely hot temperatures.

Francisco. In approximately 40 minutes they had taken control of the plane. By that time, American Flight 11 and United Flight 175 had crashed into the World Trade Center towers; thus, United 93 passengers learned of their likely fate from cell phone contact from family and friends. It is known that the passengers tried to regain control of the plane from the hijackers. In the struggle, the plane crashed in a field in Shanksville, Pennsylvania.

The fourth and final group of terrorists was the last to take off, departing from Washington, D.C., at 8:20 A.M. on American Airlines Flight 77, bound for Los Angeles. Approximately 35 minutes after takeoff, they were able to gain control of the plane and turn it around. It crashed into the Pentagon a little after 9:30 A.M.

A total of 2,992 people lost their lives as a result of these coordinated attacks on September 11, 2001. It took some time before the identities of the hijackers—and the fact that all but four of them were Saudi nationals—were confirmed, but not so with the mastermind behind the attacks. It was quickly revealed that the attacks had been ordered by a former Saudi subject, the leader of the al Qaeda network, Osama bin Laden.

## SAUDI BEGINNINGS

Osama bin Laden was one of 54 children of Muhammad bin Awad bin Laden, a poor immigrant from Yemen. He had walked from his homeland in the late 1920s, accompanied by two of his brothers, to seek his fortune. They had joined a camel caravan bound for Jeddah, a city on Saudi Arabia's Red Sea that serves as the port for passengers traveling by sea to Mecca. During the dangerous 1,000-mile journey, one of the brothers lost his life.

Muhammad bin Laden was tall and dark, blind in his right eye, and unable to read or write. But he had some training as a mason, and when he arrived in Jeddah a friend from his hometown in Yemen helped him find work, first as a porter on the waterfront, carrying cargo and passengers' belongings from the ships that arrived at the Red Sea port. Eventually, he became a bricklayer, then a handyman working at several of the Saudi royal palaces.

In the early 1930s, Muhammad bin Laden started a small construction company. The Saudi king, Abdul Aziz ibn Saud, noticed the hard work of bin Laden and his employees and soon began to hire him for various projects. Bin Laden was given the contract to build one of Saudi Arabia's first major roads, which ran from Jeddah to Medina. Later, he also built a road from Jeddah to the mountain town of Taif, where the king liked to spend the summer months. The journey that had once taken three days by camel was reduced to a mere three hours once bin Laden's firm had completed the road.

Enjoying the favor of the royal family, Muhammad bin Laden was soon the owner of the biggest contracting firm in Saudi Arabia. It was his firm that was selected to make improvements to Masjid al-Haram, in Mecca, and Masjid al-Nabawi, in Medina, two of the three holiest mosques in the Muslim faith (the third is Masjid al-Aqsa, in Jerusalem).

Muhammad bin Laden was successful in his business and in his ability to father many children. He married numerous women and, in total, had 54 children by more than 20 different mothers. He was generous with this extended family, providing all of his wives with comfortable homes, caring for his children, and bringing many of his sons into the family business.

Osama bin Laden was the seventeenth of Muhammad's 24 sons. While many of Muhammad's wives were Saudis, Osama's mother was born in Syria, where she met Muhammad in 1956. Osama was born one year later, in Riyadh. His parents soon went their separate ways, and Osama moved to Jeddah with his mother and her new husband, an employee in Muhammad bin Laden's firm.

As a young boy, Osama spent significant periods of time with his father, camping with him in the desert and learning to ride horses. Then, when he was 10 years old, his father died in a plane crash. Osama's older half brothers eventually took over the family business, continuing to be entrusted with major construction projects by the Saudi ruler and eventually developing the construction company into one of the largest in the Middle East.

At the age of 17, Osama married for the first time. His bride was his 14-year-old cousin from Syria, with whom he would have 11 children. For several years, they lived with Osama's mother and stepfather.

Osama inherited a considerable fortune from his father, but he was deeply religious, even at a young age, and extremely frugal. He studied business management at King Abdul Aziz University in Saudi Arabia. He was only a mediocre student and never graduated; instead, he spent more and more time working at the family construction business. He was a hard worker, and when Soviet troops invaded Afghanistan in 1979, he devoted his energy to fund-raising for the Afghan resistance. He also persuaded his brothers to send engineers and heavy equipment from the family firm to help build tunnels, underground hospitals, and military structures near the Afghan-Pakistani border. As a wealthy young man, he had connections among the Saudi elite and could persuade them to donate funds to support the Afghan cause.

Eventually, Osama bin Laden traveled to Afghanistan, at first briefly to visit the wounded in hospitals and provide money for needy families. By late 1986, he was part of a force of Afghan and Arab fighters who resisted a Soviet attack that included airstrikes, tanks, and paratroopers for more than 10 days.

When he returned to Saudi Arabia, bin Laden used his experiences in Afghanistan to found his own group, known as al Qaeda (Arabic for "the base"). He was in great demand as a public speaker, because he was viewed as a kind of war hero. He intended al Qaeda to be a reserve Islamic force, ready to be deployed wherever it was needed.

## TROUBLE IN THE KINGDOM

At first, bin Laden enjoyed some approval from the members of the Saudi royal family. But by late 1989, he was beginning to train a group of Yemenis to take back South Yemen, the land

Osama bin Laden *(above)* is one of the most notorious terrorists in history. Born in Saudi Arabia, he used his family's vast fortune to fund Islamic military campaigns in Afghanistan and Yemen. Accused of orchestrating terrorist attacks around the world, bin Laden has targeted his native country because of the government's diplomatic relationship with the United States.

where his father had been born. In 1990, he provided them with money and other forms of support from his base in Saudi Arabia.

When they learned of this, the Saudis did not support this effort to spark conflict in a neighboring country. They began tracking bin Laden's activities and became more concerned when he began speaking out against Iraq and its leader, Saddam

Hussein, suggesting that the al Qaeda force he was building could be used against Saddam.

On August 2, 1990, Iraqi forces swept into Kuwait and quickly occupied the country. Next, they amassed their forces along the border with Saudi Arabia, showing every sign of invading the kingdom.

Bin Laden was able to arrange a meeting with the Saudi defense minister Prince Sultan bin Abdulaziz al-Saud. (When used with the name of a tribal leader, *al* means "family of." This is different from *al* when used with a noun, as in "al Qaeda," when it means "the.") Bin Laden arrived at the meeting with maps and diagrams and began outlining his plans to use the fighting force he had amassed to combat the Iraqis. His family's construction business, he explained, could dig trenches in the sand. Above all, he argued, the kingdom must not allow a non-Islamic army to defend the land that was home to Islam's two holiest sites.

But Saudi Arabia had a long-standing relationship with the United States, and when Secretary of Defense Richard Cheney arrived in Saudi Arabia with a U.S. delegation, promising forces to defend Saudi Arabia, the kingdom was quick to accept. It was a key dividing point in the evolution of Osama bin Laden and his relationship to the leaders of his native country. From that point on, bin Laden would have two avowed enemies: the United States and the monarchy that ruled Saudi Arabia.

## ALLIES AND ENEMIES

In mid-1991, bin Laden left Saudi Arabia, traveling first to Pakistan and then to Sudan. He would never return to Saudi Arabia. On March 5, 1994, finally fed up with bin Laden's provocative statements and actions, the Saudi government formally stripped bin Laden of his citizenship, accusing him of "irresponsible behavior" and "refusal to obey instructions issued to him." His family also distanced themselves from him, expressing their regret for his actions and clearly stating that they rejected what he was saying and doing.

In Sudan, bin Laden established a haven where he began to fund a wide network of Islamic radicals. By 1996, U.S. officials had identified him as a leading terrorist and began pressuring the Sudanese government to deport him. The Saudi government, disturbed by bin Laden's increasing calls for an attack against the monarchy, did not want him returned to their country. Finally, Sudanese officials bowed to Western pressure. On May 18, 1996, they put bin Laden and his family on a plane bound for Afghanistan. At the time, U.S. officials felt it had been a wise and successful strategy—they had removed bin Laden from Sudan, where they felt he was becoming far too successful at fund-raising and arming militants. In addition, bin Laden's departure helped remove the threat to Saudi Arabia.

But it was in Afghanistan where bin Laden established firm links with the Taliban, the fundamentalist Islamic force that had seized control of the government. He set up training camps for his volunteer army and prepared numerous groups willing to die for his cause. From this new base, he would help launch attacks in Saudi Arabia, Kenya, Tanzania, Yemen, and ultimately in New York City and Washington, D.C.

The complicated relationship between the United States and Saudi Arabia entered a new phase following the attacks of September 11, 2001. Shortly after the attacks, the *New York Times* reported that Osama bin Laden had specifically requested that Saudis be recruited for the hijackings as a way to strike not only the United States but also Saudi Arabia.

Today, both the Saudi regime and U.S. officials share a growing concern about the increasing animosity among Saudi youth toward the United States and against their own rulers. Rising unemployment, decreasing opportunities, and a population boom have limited future prospects for the Saudi youth. Islamic extremism has been on the rise, and social restrictions have tightened in recent years, ensuring even more restraints on social life and more resentment against those in power. It was these factors, as well as the prolonged presence of U.S. troops on Saudi soil, that made Saudi Arabia a fertile breeding ground for al Qaeda and other recruiters seeking to enlist volunteers in the militant cause.

Bin Laden's ability to evade capture by U.S. forces also added to his reputation among al Qaeda supporters. His outspoken criticism against the Saudi royal family voiced what many in the kingdom felt but were afraid to say. He also symbolized what many believed was the core value of Wahhabism— that Islam should not merely be preserved but should be expanded.

Saudi officials had tacitly encouraged many of their young people—those most susceptible to extremist ideology—to join groups waging holy wars in other countries, no doubt as a way to turn their focus and anger away from their homeland and keep them busy on foreign soil. As they fought and trained in Afghanistan, Chechnya, Kosovo, or Bosnia, they targeted regimes other than the one ruling Saudi Arabia. In this way, al Qaeda was able to establish a recruiting network within the kingdom. It was not until after September 11, 2001, that Saudi Arabia cut its diplomatic ties to the Taliban government of Afghanistan, where thousands of Saudis had received military training.

The Kingdom of Saudi Arabia faces new challenges in the twenty-first century—challenges to adapt to shifts in the global community, security challenges, and internal challenges, particularly from its younger citizens. During the past century, a new kingdom was carved out of the sand, relationships with Western nations were transformed, and an oildependent economy was created. Clues for how Saudi Arabia will respond to the challenges of the twenty-first century can be found in its past and in the role it has played in the modern Middle East.

# 2

# Shaping a Legend

On October 30, 1918, a young British colonel was given the rare honor of a private meeting with his king. In part, King George V had agreed to the meeting out of curiosity. The young colonel, T.E. Lawrence, had gained a reputation for obtaining strategically important information in the critical area of the world we know today as the Middle East and for helping the Arabs force the Ottoman Empire's Turks from their lands. Lawrence had proven himself particularly skillful at working with the Arabs who populated the region. He had been able to provide British forces with details of key supply routes and to muster Arab support during some of the fiercest fighting of World War I.

But it was not only his expertise of the people and geography of the region that had solidified his reputation. Lawrence shunned the traditional British uniform of khakis and sun hats. Instead, he clothed himself in flowing white silk and gold-embroidered Arab robes, an astonishing image to both Europeans and Arabs alike. His wild exploits guaranteed that his reputation preceded him as he was presented to King George.

The meeting had been arranged, at least in part, as a way to honor Lawrence for his service during the war. He was to have been knighted in recognition of his outstanding military accomplishments. As King George prepared to remove the medal from its cushion and present it to the young colonel, Lawrence stopped him. He could not, he explained, accept the award, for he believed that the role he had played on behalf of the British government was dishonest. He expressed his dismay that the British government had, through him and via other channels,

T.E. Lawrence *(above)*, known in popular culture as "Lawrence of Arabia," became enamored with Arab customs and traditions when he traveled through the region on archaeological expeditions. His involvement and knowledge of local issues interested British officials, who later appointed him to work in the area on behalf of the Allied powers in World War I.

made a series of false promises to the Arab people. He now felt it was his duty to join his Arab friends in their struggle to gain the territory that had been promised them.

It was an astonishing scene; one that deeply displeased the king: a member of his own military declining a prestigious medal and, instead, expressing his disagreement with British policies in the region from which he had only recently returned. But for those who knew Lawrence, it was merely the latest chapter in a controversial and unpredictable life.

## HUMBLE BEGINNINGS

The man who would one day boldly stand before the king and express his displeasure with British policies began his life under circumstances that offered no hint of his future success. Thomas Edward Lawrence was born on August 16, 1888, in Tremadoc, a town in northern Wales. It was only when he was a teenager that he would learn that his parents had never married. Lawrence's father left his first wife and four daughters for the family's governess after she gave birth to Lawrence's older brother. Lawrence was born shortly after.

The scandal remained hidden, in part because the family moved frequently. Lawrence was the third son in a family of five boys, all born in different countries. When the family finally settled in the university town of Oxford, England, Lawrence (known as Ned when he was a boy) was eight years old. His interest in history and architecture was fostered by bicycle trips to Welsh castles and throughout parts of France. By the time he had reached the age of 20 and become an Oxford University student, he decided to take a walking tour of the region then known as the Ottoman Empire, passing through Syria, Palestine, and parts of Turkey. From July 9 until September 24, 1909, he explored cities such as Beirut, Tripoli, and Nazareth, frequently battling sickness, often walking alone. By the time his journey came to an end, he had covered nearly 1,100 miles and had become fascinated with the Middle East. He not only returned to Oxford bearing gifts of various ancient treasures he had found or purchased along the way, but he had also solidified his reputation as a fearless explorer and expert on the Middle East. Lawrence was awarded a special scholarship to perform research, and by late December 1910 he set out from England to participate in archeological expeditions, uncovering ruins in Egypt, Palestine, and Syria. For four years, Lawrence would assist several of the most noted archeologists of the time, including David Hogarth, Campbell Thompson, and Leonard Woolley. Lawrence made friends with some of the young Arabs working on the digs and began to learn their language and customs. He was known for his ability to motivate these workers—a talent that would later serve him as he became involved in British efforts to establish connections with local Arab tribes.

For Lawrence, the Arab lands in which he worked transformed his life. In the stark and serene beauty of the desert, he found a new world whose emptiness and simplicity appealed to him. The barren landscapes he excavated yielded treasures, but, more important, they provided him with a sense of purpose. He took a genuine interest in the people whose history he was uncovering. He viewed them through the prejudice of Western eyes (a sense of superiority; a need to educate them), but with one important difference: He valued their culture and did not want to see it "modernized" or transformed into some imitation of English society.

By August 1914, Lawrence's archeological assignment had come to an end, and he returned home to England. He was visiting his parents when the British government declared war on Germany. Both Great Britain and Germany had been competing to expand their influence to the Middle East, and Lawrence's knowledge of the region, his experience in remote areas, and his contacts among the Arab community made him a valuable resource. As World War I began, Lawrence was assigned to a position with the British intelligence service and posted to the Middle East.

## FALL OF AN EMPIRE

We have used the term *Middle East* to describe the region that would make Lawrence famous, but at the time he began his career in British intelligence, this part of the world was still part of the Ottoman Empire. The Ottomans were fierce warriors who had built a mighty empire that was the most powerful in the world in the late fifteenth and sixteenth centuries. The empire was so vast that for three centuries it included significant portions of Asia, Europe, and northern Africa, as well as the countries we know today as Iran, Iraq, Syria, and Saudi Arabia. It was an Islamic empire built on military conquests but relatively tolerant of the different faiths of its far-flung subjects.

The success and growth the Ottoman Empire had experienced in previous centuries was fading as the nineteenth century drew to a close. While attempts were made to modernize the empire, the sweeping changes brought about through science and technology enabled Western powers such as Great Britain to build significant empires of their own. The Ottoman Empire could no longer control the more remote regions of its territory, and these slowly began to be annexed by other countries. Independence movements began to spring up in different regions, sparked in part by the corruption of the Ottoman ruler, or sultan. Upper-class citizens of the Ottoman Empire, such as the wealthy landowners and the religious and military leaders, benefited from close ties to the sultan, including receiving an exemption from paying taxes. The vast burden of paying for the luxurious lifestyle of the sultan and his family fell on those least able to pay—the peasants, merchants, and other members of the working class.

By the time Lawrence began his first walking tour through parts of the Ottoman Empire, it was crumbling. An informal alliance had been formed between the Ottomans and Germany (many Ottoman military officers had trained in German schools), but this alliance would drag them into a war that would ultimately lead to the dissolution of the Ottoman Empire.

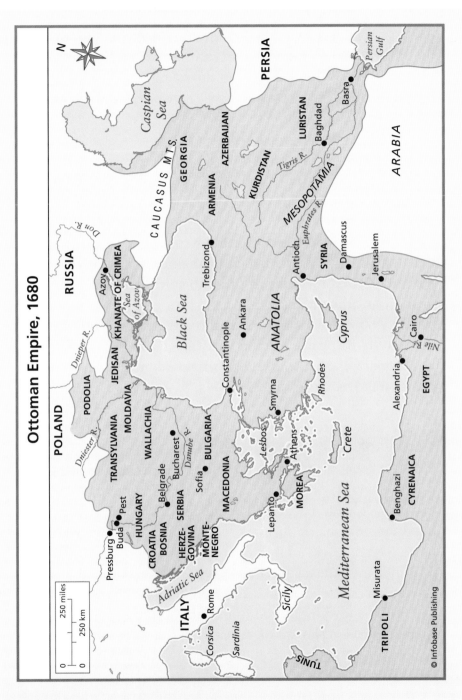

Ottoman Empire, 1680

When World War I began, the Ottoman Empire was already disintegrating from ill management and corruption. At its peak, the empire included large chunks of territory in the Balkans, northern Africa, and the Middle East.

Some of the fiercest fighting during World War I occurred on Ottoman lands. Even before the war had come to an end, the Allied Powers (particularly Great Britain and France) were making plans to carve up the Ottoman Empire. They knew that the Ottomans were weak and corrupt; they would not leave the region's fate to chance.

As early as 1914, foreign ministers from Great Britain and France had signed a series of treaties that revealed their plans to carve up the parts of the Ottoman Empire that stretched across the Middle East. One of these treaties, signed in May 1916, was known as the Sykes-Picot Agreement. It would cause a stir when its contents were finally revealed, demonstrating that the Allied Powers had been making plans to carve up the Middle East for years in order to suit their own needs. In most cases, these plans ignored the thoughts or wishes of the people who lived there. Among those worried by this display of Western arrogance was the British intelligence officer who was encouraging an Arab revolt that would greatly assist British plans—T.E. Lawrence.

## ARAB REVOLT

By 1916, some British military efforts focused on securing the most vulnerable portions of the Ottoman Empire by establishing contact with tribal and religious leaders in strategically important regions. In this way, military officials hoped to open up supply routes, as well as to enlist the local tribes in fighting for Allied interests against the Ottoman forces. In these efforts, Lawrence's contacts and skills proved highly valuable. In October 1916, he was dispatched from Cairo to the region known as Arabia. A revolt was taking place—Arab armies were fighting against the Ottoman forces, battling for their freedom and a land of their own.

This was a positive development for the British, who did all they could to encourage the Arab revolt to take pressure off their own troops who were battling the Ottomans in the Sinai Desert and the Suez Canal region. They had little intention of granting independence to those who were under Ottoman control, but they did not reveal this to the Arabs.

Instead, Lawrence was sent off to meet with representatives from the Arab armies, in part to determine who could best assist the British in their efforts to defeat Ottoman forces in the region. Lawrence's unwillingness to mince words made his reports useful, and occasionally entertaining, as he dismissed one potential leader after another, listing an assortment of faults—from their excessive ambition to their inability to think and act independently.

Following a 100-mile journey on camel, under the heat of the Arabian sun, Lawrence at last found the man he thought could best lead the Arab revolt (and serve British interests). The Arabian *sheikh* (a title of respect, often translated as "leader" but literally meaning "old man") Faisal ibn Hussein impressed Lawrence with his height and intelligence, with the way he commanded his men, and with his forceful opinions. Lawrence would soon join forces with Faisal, wearing Arab clothes and participating in the tribal revolt that would contribute to the war's end and the collapse of Ottoman control of the region. He gained a reputation for bravery, an admirable trait among the fierce Arab tribes. Although he was wounded many times, he continued to fight, leading a team of Arabs into the desert and repeatedly engaging the Ottoman forces, freeing up British forces to invade Syria and Palestine.

In detailed letters to senior military officials, Lawrence described the incredible picture this Arab force made as it moved across the stark Arabian landscape: Faisal in front, dressed in sparkling white robes, with Lawrence on his left, clothed in bright red and white. Behind them flew three purple silk banners on long poles with gold spikes at the top. Next came three drummers playing a march, and behind them came 1,200 camels, packed with supplies and bouncing close together, and a troop of men wearing brightly colored clothing and all loudly singing a battle song praising Faisal and his family.

Faisal I *(above center)* first served in World War I with the Ottoman army but later fled to join his father and brothers in the Arab revolt against the Ottoman Empire. With the help of T.E. Lawrence *(middle row, second right)*, Faisal fought for Arab nationalism and independence in the Middle East, and was briefly proclaimed king of Syria, and later Iraq.

It is not surprising that, by the time the war had ended, Lawrence had become famous. But he was also a man with a troubled conscience. He knew that he had betrayed the land and the men who had made him a celebrity. The Arabs under Faisal had fought fiercely for their independence—and the independence of all Arabs. But Great Britain had different plans. The lands of the Middle East would protect the direct route between Great Britain and its most treasured possession, India.

And so it was a conflicted Lawrence who was granted the honor of a meeting with his king and who refused the military award offered to him. While his own future now looked promising, the future of the land he had left behind seemed very uncertain.

# 3

# The House of Saud

The history of the country we know today as Saudi Arabia is, in many ways, the history of one family—a family known by the name al-Saud. This family united a desert land governed by many different sheikhs and rulers into a single country. Then, with the discovery of oil beneath that desert sand, the family helped the country become an economic power.

Their story, which illustrates the creation of Saudi Arabia, began as the nineteenth century drew to a close, in the bleak desert sand of the southeastern part of Arabia, a land so forbidding that it was known as the Empty Quarter. Moving through that desert landscape was a small displaced clan—the Saud family. During the early nineteenth century, they had been one of the most powerful families in Arabia, controlling the holy cities of Mecca and Medina and dominating a vast stretch of land from Yemen to Syria, from the Red Sea to the Persian Gulf.

But this time of power lasted little more than 12 years. The Ottoman rulers in Constantinople were threatened by the family's holdings (Ottoman legitimacy rested in part on the possession of the Muslim holy cities), and the twin holy cities were soon recaptured. The people fought fiercely against the Ottoman army, but ultimately the leader of the Saud family was forced to surrender. He was transported to Constantinople, where his head was cut off and his headless body displayed as a warning to any other rebellious citizens.

The Saud family left behind the shattered remains of their palaces and relocated, this time to Riyadh. Here, their dreams were not as grand, and for nearly a century they ruled over a smaller region. But this territory, too, would soon be snatched away, in yet another series of bloody battles, this time with the al-Rashid, a family aligned with the Ottoman Empire.

The Saud family, seeking shelter in the inhospitable Empty Quarter, seemed to have been defeated. They led a nomadic life by living in tents made of black goat hair and traveling on camels. They moved south in the heat of the summer, seeking water and grazing land for their animals. Among the members of the Saud family who grew up in this harsh climate was a young teenager named Abdul Aziz ibn Saud.

Abdul Aziz studied the ways of the Bedouins, the nomads with whom he lived. Lacking a permanent home, he slept at night in the open and had no luxuries. His blanket was made of rough wool from camel's hair. The camels the tribe rode and used were their most prized possessions. The stories Abdul Aziz learned while he was growing up seemed like fairy tales— legends of a time when his family had once been one of the strongest in all of Arabia.

But as Abdul Aziz grew older, he became firmly convinced that his life had a single purpose: to restore his family's honor, to recapture the land it had once held, and to return the Saud family to the highest position in Arabia.

For a while, these hopes were just the dreams of a restless teenager. For two years, Abdul Aziz lived in the desert with his family, absorbing the lessons of the Bedouins with whom the family traveled. He learned self-confidence—the kind of poise that comes with carving a living out of the harshest conditions, of forgoing all luxuries, of sleeping in the open. He learned the importance of the unit, rather than the individual, by watching the Bedouin caravans transport men, women, and children, plus all their necessary supplies, on camels for long distances through the desert.

In 1890, the Saud family took refuge in the port city of Kuwait, where they stayed for several years. It was a humble existence in a mud house with only three rooms in a damp and smelly back alley. Abdul Aziz was a good Muslim, and following the tradition of the time he married early, at the age of 16.

Abdul Aziz ibn Saud (1880–1953) regained control of Najd in 1922, the interior highlands of Arabia, an area that had been historically maintained by his family but lost to the rival al-Rashid dynasty. He conquered the Hijaz in 1925, then renamed these lands Saudi Arabia in 1932 and proclaimed himself king. Oil was later discovered in Saudi Arabia, and upon his death in 1953, he was one of the richest men in the world.

Unfortunately, the cramped family quarters and dampness of their home proved fatal to Abdul Aziz's young wife, and only six months after their marriage she died.

In later years, Abdul Aziz would disdain the six years he lived in Kuwait, but it was while the family struggled to survive in the port city that the Saudis came to realize that they might recapture some of their past glory. At that time, the ruler of Kuwait was a sheikh named Mubarak al-Sabah, and he was always trying to strengthen Kuwait—and his position as ruler in the process. Today, we think of Kuwait as one of the wealthiest countries in the world, owing to its vast oil resources. But at the time Abdul Aziz and his family lived there, Kuwait was viewed as little more than a port—one in which goods from abroad passed into central Arabia.

Sheikh Mubarak decided that the easiest way to maintain Kuwait's importance was to make sure that the rest of Arabia was weaker. And this could best be accomplished by dividing it. Sheikh Mubarak felt that the al-Rashid had become too confident. It was time to test their power—and to make sure that they did not entertain any thoughts of invading Kuwait. He needed to divert the attention of the al-Rashid, so he decided that the perfect diversion would be a new attack on Riyadh by the Saud family.

Sheikh Mubarak began to meet with Abdul Aziz and to help him shape a more realistic plan for restoring his family's honor and glory. As the young man spent more and more time with his mentor, they created a plan that would lead Abdul Aziz back to Arabia and turn the Saud family's dreams of a return to power into reality.

## THE BATTLE BEGINS

In the early part of 1901, Sheikh Mubarak directed an army of Bedouins, with members of the Saud family in their midst, to attack a section of Rashidi territory around Ha'il. Their forces were soundly defeated, and in response the al-Rashid launched their own attack on Mubarak's Kuwaiti territory.

But the Rashidi's plan to conquer Kuwait alarmed the British. Sheikh Mubarak had been willing to allow British ships access to the Kuwaiti port. The al-Rashid might prove friendlier to German interests because of Germany's close ties with the Ottoman Empire. So British ships quickly steamed into the Kuwaiti harbor, and British forces joined the Mubarak army to turn back the invaders.

Kuwait was safe. Suddenly Abdul Aziz recognized that the time had come to launch his own attack. The Rashidi forces, dismayed at their unexpected defeat, were far from Riyadh, still focusing on Mubarak's challenge. Their distraction offered a chance for a surprise attack, and Abdul Aziz was determined to seize it.

He was only 21 years old, but he had been planning this moment for a long time. He gathered together a party of about 40 men, including his half brother Muhammad and several of his cousins. They were determined to recapture Riyadh and restore their family honor, or die trying.

The party rode south and west on camels in September 1901, trying to gather support for the attack as they traveled. Gradually, their numbers increased, until about 200 men gathered south of Riyadh in preparation for the battle. But as Abdul Aziz made plans to launch his attack, his hope for a quick victory began to fade. He learned that his plans for a surprise attack had somehow been leaked to the al-Rashid, who had busily set about fortifying the city. The weather had turned, growing cold at night and making sleeping in the desert a difficult and uncomfortable prospect. Abdul Aziz's followers, who had been promised a quick fight and sudden riches, lost interest at the prospect of a prolonged battle and because there were few provisions to fortify them during the battle. Gradually, his fighting force began to slip away, until Abdul Aziz found himself in charge of no more than 60 or 70 men.

Abdul Aziz then gathered his small force together and explained the dangers they faced. He did not intend to return to Kuwait in defeat, but he offered his men the chance to return home. Instead, they chose to fight with him—to the death.

With this small band of faithful men, Abdul Aziz plotted the only strategy that gave them a chance. They retreated from Riyadh, heading south. And there, they disappeared, hiding in the desert. To the Rashidi soldiers stationed at Riyadh, it seemed as if the al-Saud army had given up and headed back to Kuwait.

For 50 days, Abdul Aziz and his men hid in the Empty Quarter—the very desert where he had first learned the ways of the Bedouins. He used his lessons well. During those long days, he and his men rested. At night, under cover of darkness, they crept out of their hiding places to drink and eat whatever they could find. Then, sweeping away any traces of their footsteps, they slipped back into hiding.

Finally, on the night of January 15, 1902, the time had come for them to make their desperate attempt to win back the Saud family's honor. As darkness spread over Riyadh, Abdul Aziz and his men walked quietly out of the desert. Carrying the few weapons they had—some swords and daggers, a rifle or two—they stealthily approached the unsuspecting guards patrolling the city's walls. A small scouting party of about six men, including Abdul Aziz, quickly climbed over the wall and headed for the garrison where the Rashidi army kept its supplies and weapons.

Their first stop was the governor's house, just across the street from the garrison. They tied up the governor's wife, and then one man crept back to the troops to bring reinforcements. They gathered quietly, waiting for the sun to rise, when the governor would emerge from his base at the garrison and head back to his home across the street for breakfast. Finally, after several hours, they saw the governor appear and cross the street to his home.

Abdul Aziz wasted no time. He charged the governor, who immediately attempted to return to the garrison. But the governor was too late. Abdul Aziz tackled him, and the rest of the al-Saud forces swiftly joined him, fighting off the governor's guards, who were attempting to pull the governor back into the garrison. But Abdul Aziz held him tight. This tug-of-war went on for several seconds, until the governor managed to free himself and was pulled inside.

The quick thinking of one of Abdul Aziz's cousins saved the day. He entered the garrison and managed to get off a shot that killed the governor. In a matter of minutes, the battle was over. Abdul Aziz's forces had triumphed. The men in the garrison surrendered, and Abdul Aziz took charge of Riyadh. The Saud family once more controlled the very heart of Arabia.

## THE BEGINNING OF A KINGDOM

The al-Rashid had been fierce and tyrannical rulers of Riyadh and the surrounding territories, using methods that had proved effective while in power but that were quickly used against them once a portion of their territory began to slip away. The Bedouins who lived in the deserts surrounding Riyadh were delighted to learn that the Rashidi rulers had been overthrown. They quickly traveled to Riyadh to see the young victor whose father had once ruled them, and to promise their loyalty.

Their pledges to serve Abdul Aziz were valuable. At the time, Arabia was ruled by an assembly of sheikhs whose territories were not reflected by clear boundaries but by the number of Bedouins who agreed to support them and by where the sheiks grazed and watered their flocks. Abdul Aziz had captured Riyadh, but retaking the land beyond the city—the full extent of the territory retaken by the Saud family—depended largely on which Bedouin tribes agreed to accept him as their *emir*, or leader.

The extent of the land controlled by Abdul Aziz was still to be determined, but one thing was certain—this new kingdom was surrounded by enemies. The al-Rashid had been driven back to the north, where they would surely reassemble and try to retake Riyadh. The east, containing valuable access to the Persian Gulf, was controlled by the Ottoman Empire. In the west, where the holy cities of Mecca and Medina were located, was a vast stretch of land known as the Hijaz, controlled by the sharif of Mecca. This was the greatest prize of all Arabia, because the Hijaz held both religious and financial value. For faithful Muslims, the pilgrimage, or *hajj*, to Mecca is one of the

As a religious duty noted in the Koran, all healthy men and women who are financially able must perform the hajj, the major pilgrimage to Mecca. Over 2 million Muslims from more than 70 countries visit Mecca every year to pray at the Kaaba *(above)*, a black rectangular shrine inside the Grand Mosque, Islam's holiest shrine.

most important tenets of their religion. At least once in his life, a devout Muslim—if he is physically and financially able—is expected to go to Mecca. The annual rites surrounding this pilgrimage, with the arrival of tens of thousands of faithful Muslims, made Mecca a very wealthy city indeed. Mecca was a gathering place—a city where Muslims from many different countries came together not only to worship but to trade goods and share ideas.

As Abdul Aziz examined the land captured by his family, one thing became clear. He had only one ally: Mubarak al-Sabah, in the northeastern port of Kuwait. Abdul Aziz needed more allies if he was going to hold on to Riyadh, and he needed them quickly.

As Bedouin leaders continued to arrive to pledge their loyalty, Abdul Aziz ordered his forces to repair the city's walls in preparation for an attack. He sent for his family, and the arrival of his father was greeted with enthusiastic cheers. But there was little debate about who was the leader of the Saud family. Abdul Aziz's father publicly declared that he was stepping down in favor of his son, presenting him with a magnificent sword as a symbol of the transfer of power from one generation to the next.

Abdul Aziz wasted little time basking in the praise he received from the people of Riyadh, or in the admiration of the Bedouins. He knew that he had to assemble a stronger army and defend the city from those who wanted to take it back. He soon returned to the desert, heading south in search of fighters to join his side.

Abdul Aziz was young, but his physique was impressive, as he stood nearly six foot three, much taller than most of the other Bedouins. He had the noble heritage of the Saud family, and the glory of his recent success in Riyadh. But this was about all he had. He needed something to attract a new group of followers to his cause. He could not offer them money; his family had almost none. But he believed that his cause was just and that it was a holy quest. It was through this conviction that he found the source for his new army.

## A NEW CRUSADE

In the desert surrounding Riyadh lived a group who practiced a particularly strict form of Islam. They did not drink or smoke; they shunned rich foods and fine clothing, believing that most worldly comforts and pleasures were sinful. They were known as

Wahhabis (they do not use this term themselves), named after the man (Muhammad ibn Abd al-Wahhab) who had proclaimed, during the eighteenth century, their strict interpretation of the Sharia, the rules and laws of Islam based on the Koran and the recorded sayings and actions of the Prophet Muhammad. Wahhab had been protected by the Saud family in the mid-1700s, and the relationship had benefited both sides and led to a lasting alliance. Wahhab had preached a philosophy of reform and conversion—that it was the duty of good Muslims not merely to shape their own lives to follow the rules of the Koran but also to ensure that their neighbors did as well. Wahhabis believed that devotion to Islam should exceed tribal loyalty. Muslims, they felt, were part of a worldwide community of believers, not simply an isolated tribe of faithful worshippers. For the Wahhabis, Muslims who did not share their views were no better than unbelievers—they were enemies of God. If preaching and sharing their experiences was not enough, then they would convert other Muslims to their faith by force. This sense of engaging in a holy war became the motivation for the Saud family to move out from their base into other parts of Arabia in the eighteenth century. By the beginning of the nineteenth century, the al-Saud, united and inspired by Wahhabi teaching, had taken control of Mecca and Medina and ruled a vast empire.

Although this earlier Saudi Empire did not last into the twentieth century, the link between the al-Saud and the Wahhabis had not been forgotten. As Abdul Aziz began to plan a way to reinforce his army, he naturally thought of the fiercely determined Wahhabis. He decided that it was time for him to get married again. The bride he chose was the daughter of Riyadh's leading religious authority, the chief of the Muslim legal experts known as the *ulama*. He also happened to be a direct descendent of Muhammad ibn Abd al-Wahhab.

For seven months, Abdul Aziz built up an army, courting the ulama by granting them the authority to set all laws in Riyadh and oversee all questions of morality. He rode into the desert, to meet with the Bedouin leaders. He ate and prayed with them and even slept outdoors with them. He needed as much support as he could get, because word had reached him that the al-Rashid were threatening to retake the land they had lost.

The battle came not in Riyadh, with its newly fortified walls, but in a small settlement south of the city. There, Abdul Aziz had stationed his men among the palm trees, ordering them to lie still, hiding behind their camel saddles. They watched and waited for the Rashidi forces to move into the open.

This would seem like a straightforward approach to battle, but to the Bedouins the strategy was revolutionary. The Rashidi forces had never encountered an enemy who fought from fixed positions, so they had no reason to be cautious as they rode forward into the open. However, as they reached the palm groves, they were immediately fired upon. The bursts of rifle fire continued all day, and ultimately the Rashidi forces were forced to retreat.

The next day, Abdul Aziz's men once more resumed their position, but to their surprise they saw the Rashidi forces packing up and moving out. There would be no second day of fighting, which the al-Saud forces welcomed. For what the Rashidi army did not realize was that Abdul Aziz's troops had used up nearly every last bit of ammunition during the battle. They could not have fought another day. But the Rashidi army had given up, and once more Abdul Aziz's forces had triumphed.

As news of his two victories traveled from settlement to settlement, Abdul Aziz soon found his territory expanding as more tribal leaders arrived to pledge their loyalty. Only a year and a half after he had first launched his attack on Riyadh, he was in control of a region that stretched a hundred miles to the north and a hundred miles to the south of the city that would become the capital of his new kingdom.

## A KINGDOM RESTORED

By the spring of 1904, the al-Rashid realized that the threat posed by Abdul Aziz and the Saudi army might be much greater than they originally had thought. Now that the Saudis had successfully won back so much of their old territory, it was only a matter of time before they began to think about conquering the land traditionally held by the al-Rashid as well. The al-Rashid turned to the powerful Ottoman army for assistance. Abdul Aziz wasted little time turning to his own ally. He sent a request for help and supplies to the representative of the British Empire in the Persian Gulf, a man named Percy Cox.

Sir Percy Cox served in the British military and was assigned to various posts throughout the Middle East in the early twentieth century. When Abdul Aziz needed reinforcements and supplies in his campaign against the combined forces of the Rashidi and Ottoman armies, the British sent Cox. *Above*, Cox *(center)* stands with British diplomat and archaeologist Gertrude Bell *(right)* and King Faisal I *(left)* of Iraq.

Cox genuinely admired the Arabs and knew about the political situation in Arabia. He could speak Arabic and was trusted by the Arabs. He also had built a friendship with Abdul Aziz's old friend and mentor from Kuwait, Sheikh Mubarak. The British had proved a useful ally and protector to Mubarak and Kuwait, sending in warships to the Kuwaiti ports just as the Ottomans seemed poised to attack. Perhaps they would be willing to provide the same defensive support to the Saud family.

Percy Cox and a number of other British politicians wanted to assist the Saud family, but some British politicians supported the Rashidi faction, believing that British interests in Arabia should go no further than the coastal areas. For several months, these competing factions exchanged letters and telegrams debating their respective opinions. While the correspondence went back and forth between various British offices, Abdul Aziz ran out of time. In early 1904, the Ottoman forces pledged their support to the army of the Rashidi faction. Shortly thereafter, Abdul Aziz's forces assembled in the desert east of Anayzah, only a short distance from their enemies.

The Ottomans had brought an advantage to the Rashidi side: artillery. Abdul Aziz's fighters were fierce Bedouin warriors, but they had never encountered artillery fire, so the first battle ended in a Saudi retreat, with their leader wounded in his hand and leg. The only thing that saved them from complete defeat was the fact that they were used to fighting in the desert heat. The Ottoman forces were not. As the heat of summer beat down on the two camps, the Ottoman soldiers, unaccustomed to the desert and having marched hundreds of miles to reach the site of the battle, were suffering.

After that initial battle, the two sides were essentially stalemated. For several weeks, neither side moved. Both armies had become afflicted with cholera and had no desire to fight. In the end, it was the Rashidi forces that made the first move. Their fighters finally decided that they would leave for home. The Saudi army caught them as they attempted to sneak away one night, and they were quickly overwhelmed; the Ottoman forces were also soon overpowered.

While the victory was significant, the more important prize was the Ottoman artillery the Saudis captured. But Abdul Aziz understood that the vast Ottoman Empire had many more troops to dispatch into the desert, and he had no desire to fight against a superior force. He decided that the time had come for diplomacy, so he sent his father to serve as his representative to the Ottomans. The negotiations were ultimately successful, and by 1905 Ottoman authorities had agreed to recognize the Saud family's rightful possession of the territory they had retaken. In exchange, Abdul Aziz agreed to serve as the Ottoman district commissioner for the territory, in effect agreeing to submit to Ottoman sovereignty over his land.

It was not an arrangement that would last long. By the spring of 1906, the forces of Abdul Aziz once again fought the Rashidi army, and once more defeated them, this time killing the head of the family. Chaos ensued among the al-Rashid, as various relatives competed to become the new tribal leader. With northern Arabia caught up in intrigue and chaos, Abdul Aziz had little to fear from the Rashidi forces. He no longer needed his Ottoman alliance. His tribes were soon raiding Ottoman supply caravans, and before long the Ottoman army, crippled by defectors and political problems in Constantinople, began to pull out of central Arabia.

In only a few years, Abdul Aziz had gained firm control of a large stretch of Arabian territory. Having successfully defeated the Rashidi forces in the north, and having outlasted the Ottoman forces, he began to focus his efforts on western Arabia. The holy cities of Mecca and Medina had once been part of the Saudi Empire. As a devout Muslim, Abdul Aziz felt a divine call to return them to the protection of the Saud family.

# 4

# King of Arabia

In the spring of 1910, Abdul Aziz was 30 years old. He arrived in Kuwait to visit his old friend Sheikh Mubarak. By then, the British fully understood how powerful Abdul Aziz was becoming, so the British political representative in Kuwait, a man named Captain William Shakespear (a distant descendant of the English poet and playwright), decided to invite him to dinner. Captain Shakespear was impressed by Abdul Aziz's openness.

It was during a second meeting that Abdul Aziz explained his plans. He had determined to recapture the province of Al-Hasa, which lay along the eastern coast of the Persian Gulf and had been seized by the Ottomans in 1871.

If he had expected the British representative to offer his support or encouragement, he was disappointed. Captain Shakespear explained that Great Britain had a good relationship with the Ottoman Empire and had no wish to participate in an attack against it. At a meeting two months later, the subject came up again. By now, the Ottoman Empire was crumbling, and its armies were being pulled back closer and closer to Turkey to hold onto the remaining bits of territory. At the time, other Ottoman subjects were gaining their independence, so Abdul Aziz was determined that Arabia would join this group.

Captain Shakespear once more cautioned Abdul Aziz against any attack, explaining that Great Britain would not be able to support his efforts. He then sent a report of the meeting to his superiors, convinced that Abdul Aziz understood that an attack would be disastrous. But on the same day that Shakespear sent the report, he learned that Saudi troops had captured Al-Hasa. A significant portion of the Persian Gulf coast now belonged to

Abdul Aziz; it would one day prove to be some of the most valuable land on Earth.

Great Britain soon had to reassess the somewhat dismissive attitude it had initially adopted in considering an alliance with Abdul Aziz. Not long after Abdul Aziz successfully seized Al-Hasa, Great Britain found itself opposing the Ottoman Empire as World War I began. Suddenly, the strategic importance of Arabia became a paramount concern, as both sides quickly attempted to establish themselves in the region to ensure safe passage of their ships and supplies. When it became clear that the Rashidi forces had united with the Ottomans (who signed a secret treaty alliance with Germany), Great Britain suddenly became very interested in the plans of Abdul Aziz.

Captain Shakespear was drafted into service once more, this time to try to persuade Abdul Aziz to agree to an alliance quite similar to the one he himself had proposed several months earlier. But Abdul Aziz, having been turned down twice before, was no longer eager to attach himself to the British. As Shakespear attempted to plead the British cause, Abdul Aziz's attention was focused elsewhere—on an imminent battle with the Rashidi forces north of Riyadh. Abdul Aziz urged Shakespear to leave the camp quickly, because the pending battle was certain to be bloody and fierce. But Shakespear knew that the battle would have strategic significance for the larger war being fought. If the Rashidi army—linked with the Ottomans—should lose, Great Britain would be in a much stronger position in the Middle East. It was an opportunity to witness a potentially historic battle, and Shakespear decided to stay.

But the victory Shakespear had hoped to witness did not happen. Instead, the Saudi forces were quickly overpowered and fled. Shakespear was shot and died on the battlefield, and as a result of this defeat, Abdul Aziz determined that his Saudi forces would play no role in the unfolding conflict that would become World War I.

The battle marked another critical turning point as well. Shakespear had pleaded the cause of Abdul Aziz to his superiors, and they had considered the possibility of an alliance with the Saudi leader as a way to cement British ties to the Arab world. But after Shakespear's death, another British subject, also skilled at forming relationships with the Bedouins, would have tremendous influence on the course of Great Britain's association with the Arabs. His name was T.E. Lawrence, and he had a very different candidate in mind to be the leader of the Arab revolt: the third son of the sharif of Mecca, Faisal bin Hussein.

## A WEAKENED EMPIRE

It seems tempting, with the wisdom of hindsight, to argue that Great Britain should have devoted more support to Abdul Aziz, rather than to Faisal bin Hussein. But as World War I unfolded, Abdul Aziz was busy with his own problems and in no position to assist the British in their efforts to spark an Arab revolt against the Ottoman Empire. A group of rebellious sheikhs were attempting to wrest parts of their land away from the Saudi Empire. This group had no interest in paying taxes to support the Saudi family in distant Riyadh, and they eventually forced a series of disastrous battles. At the time that T. E. Lawrence was building his own reputation, assisting Faisal's forces in overpowering the vastly superior Ottoman armies, Abdul Aziz was simply fighting to hold on to what he had.

It was a subdued Abdul Aziz who finally agreed to meet with Percy Cox in December 1915 to conclude the discussions that had been initiated by Captain Shakespear. Both sides left the meeting satisfied with their new Anglo-Saudi friendship treaty. Great Britain was granted trading privileges and oversight of Saudi foreign policy. Abdul Aziz received a guarantee of British protection against Saudi enemies and much-needed weapons and money. Within a year, the influx of supplies and money enabled Abdul Aziz to stamp out any rebellions and begin the process of setting up an independent Saudi state in central Arabia.

With central Arabia firmly in hand, Abdul Aziz was becoming a valuable ally of the British, but the flaunting of power by another British ally—the sharif of Mecca—was beginning to annoy him. Sharif Hussein bin Ali had gone so far as to declare himself the "king of all Arabs," but Abdul Aziz had little intention of sharing his empire with anyone.

## THE MAN WHO WOULD BE KING

Sharif Hussein sought British support to ensure the continuance of his kingdom in Arabia for several years, but prior to their alliance he had relied on the support and favor of the Ottoman Empire. It was due to the Ottoman rulers in Constantinople that he had been granted the right to govern Mecca and Medina, as well as the region of Arabia known as the Hijaz. His family claimed to be descended from the Prophet Muhammad, but it was his relationship with the Ottomans, more than his family lineage, that had placed him in charge of this prized region of Arabia.

As we have seen from the story of T. E. Lawrence, British leaders spent much of the time before and after World War I carving up the Middle East and choosing rulers who would ultimately uphold British interests while attempting to suppress any opposition in the mold of the Ottoman Empire. As they studied the competing rivals—Abdul Aziz and Sharif Hussein—they understood that they were choosing between central and western Arabia. Both men had family ties that had linked them to Arabian soil for generations. Both men were eager to build an alliance with the British to ensure that they remained in power. And both men ultimately hoped to rule all of Arabia. But that was essentially where the similarities ended.

Sharif Hussein was approximately 20 years older than Abdul Aziz, and he was no desert Bedouin. He was a city dweller, and the heart of his kingdom was in the bustling urban centers of Mecca, Medina, and Jeddah. Unlike Abdul Aziz, whose kingdom was in need of money, Sharif Hussein ruled over a territory whose economy was thriving, largely due to the annual influx of Muslim pilgrims coming to Mecca. Much of Mecca's

Sharif Hussein *(above, in black hat)* was chosen by the British to lead the Arab Revolt against the Ottoman Empire. Chosen over the veteran fighter Abdul Aziz, Hussein's location in Islam's holiest cities, Mecca and Medina, was a strategic advantage in uniting Arabs from other countries like Syria and Palestine.

economy was based on providing supplies and shelter to the pilgrims, generally at highly inflated prices. The luxuries available in Mecca were abhorrent to Abdul Aziz's Wahhabi supporters. They believed that the unofficial capital of the Muslim faith needed to be reformed.

The two men were as different in temperament and personality as the territories they ruled. Both were clever men, but whereas Abdul Aziz was known for being frank and outspoken, Sharif Hussein delighted in puzzling the British who courted him, and many frustrated diplomats would leave his presence uncertain whether their meeting had been a success.

The British ultimately chose to back Sharif Hussein, although competing forces within their government quarreled bitterly over the choice. But there were several valid arguments for supporting the sharif of Mecca over the ruler of central Arabia.

First was the simple fact of geography. Central Arabia was almost inaccessible before the advent of air travel and largely unknown to the majority of British administrators in the region. The advantage Sharif Hussein's kingdom offered—access to the Red Sea—provided strategic value. His title—sharif of Mecca—underscored the fact that he was in control of what many Muslims viewed as the most important city of all. His position as guardian of the holy city meant that he could offer potential leadership, not only to the Muslims of Arabia but to Muslims throughout the world.

Great Britain's goal was to spark an Arab revolt against the Ottomans. They hoped for this rebellion to take place throughout all of the former Ottoman territories, especially Arabia, Syria, Iraq, and Palestine. Sharif Hussein's family ties stretched beyond Mecca and Medina to include connections in Turkey, Syria, and Palestine. All of this made him the logical candidate for Great Britain to back, and so they did.

It was a bitter disappointment to Abdul Aziz. But he did not abandon his dreams of creating a united Arabia under Saudi leadership. Instead, he turned elsewhere for assistance, to a group of tribes living about 160 miles from Riyadh. He united them into a single fighting force—designed to support him—and they soon became known as the *Ikhwan* (the Brotherhood).

The Ikhwan were linked to the Wahhabis in that they believed in living their life in complete accordance with the teachings of the Koran and the Hadith (the collection of words and deeds of Muhammad). Abdul Aziz had supported the Ikhwan, giving them land, weapons, supplies, and even encouraging new missionaries to join with the Ikhwan's crusade to convert the Bedouins.

It was an investment that would prove very wise, because as World War I began to wind down, Abdul Aziz knew that the supplies Great Britain had given Sharif Hussein to overthrow the Ottomans might soon be turned against Riyadh. The sharif had not proclaimed himself "king of all Arabs" for nothing, and Abdul Aziz knew that the Saudi territory was one of the few remaining obstacles to Sharif Hussein's effort to claim the entire peninsula as his own.

A basic tenet of the Ikhwan philosophy was the strong opposition to Western materialistic culture. Singing and dancing were banned; most children's games were banned; smoking, radios, and telephones were banned; even gold, silk, and jewelry were considered out of step with the teachings of Muhammad.

In this austere setting, Abdul Aziz saw opportunity. Many of the Ikhwan were Bedouins, used to life in the desert and the practice of raiding other camps for supplies. They were not urban priests, preaching a message of faith in comfortable settings and urging their followers to abstain from the temptations surrounding them. These were militants who believed that anyone killed in a holy war would be transported to Paradise, because their death would have been for a just and noble cause. And they were well armed for their cause.

By 1917, the Ikhwan had spread throughout the Najd region of central Arabia. They had more than 200 settlements, and within those settlements about 60,000 men of fighting age were prepared to go into battle, provided it was for a holy cause.

Abdul Aziz had an entire army at his disposal. He only needed to determine how and when to use it.

He did not have long to wait. Within a year, World War I ended. Confident of British support, Sharif Hussein had determined that the time had come to cement his hold over all of Arabia. He sent a force, headed by his son Abdullah, to subdue the regions that lay between Mecca and Riyadh—a territory known

Abdul Aziz knew an alliance with the Ikhwan would prove beneficial to his future plans of forming a united Arab country under his leadership. Fervently religious and dedicated to the basic tenets of Islam, the Ikhwan are fierce warriors who have spurned aspects of Western culture. *Above*, a modern-day pro-India group that has taken the name Ikhwan was formed in 1994 by Pakistani military commander Mohammed Yusuf.

as Kurmah—in part because those lands had recently become the targets of Ikhwan missionaries. It quickly became clear that Abdullah had no intention of stopping once he had taken Kurmah; instead, he planned to seize Riyadh and continue until he had captured all Saudi territory.

Abdullah did not think he would have to deal with the Ikhwan. But stories of the brave fighting of the Ikhwan missionaries in Kurmah, struggling against Abdullah's forces, had sparked the fury of the Ikhwan militia. Their fellow believers were in danger—a clear call for holy war.

The Ikhwan could travel for hundreds of miles with minimal supplies. They were fierce fighters who believed that they were on a mission from God. They moved swiftly across the desert on camels, and when they found Abdullah's forces asleep, they immediately began killing every man they could find. For them, Paradise was the ultimate goal, so they were completely fearless in battle. By the time the sun rose, only a handful of men (including Abdullah) had escaped.

The Ikhwan were ready to move on to Mecca, which would have been essentially defenseless without Abdullah's forces to block their advance. But Abdul Aziz did not want to conquer Mecca. He saw the holy city as a piece of a much larger empire, one that needed to be built on rightful leadership as much as on conquest. So the Ikhwan returned to their settlements, and Abdul Aziz continued to wait for the right time to claim his larger prize.

## THE END OF THE AL-RASHIDS

It was not easy to subdue the Ikhwan, once they had been called to battle. But it was not long before Abdul Aziz summoned his troops again. By 1920, the al-Rashid's own internal power struggle had reached a deadly climax, with the ruler shot dead by his cousin, who was quickly executed. It had been a difficult task to control the kingdom, as one after another of the heirs were killed in battle with the Saudis or by members of their own family. The sole survivor of this deadly tussle was an 18-year-old boy whose mother was a slave.

Abdul Aziz knew that the weakened kingdom could not face a serious challenge and that its people might be looking for a more inspiring ruler than the son of a slave. And he was correct. Within three weeks, the war between the Rashidi forces and the Saudis—a war that had lasted on and off for 20 years—was over. The kingdom belonged to Abdul Aziz.

Abdul Aziz had triumphed once more. But the newly proclaimed sultan, who came to be known as Ibn Saud (son of Saud), would have to deal with a new set of problems—most of which dealt with the British.

In a meeting in Cairo, Egypt, held in March 1921, Winston Churchill, the British secretary of state for the colonies, decided the time had finally come to resolve the status of the Middle East. He collected a group of experts—which included T.E. Lawrence—and gave them the task of deciding how best to carve up the Middle East.

It was an astounding example of Western arrogance. The conference of "Middle Eastern experts" consisted of 35 Englishmen (and one woman—Gertrude Bell) and only two Arabs (both aides to Sharif Hussein's son Faisal). It was not surprising that members of the conference determined that the former territories of the Ottoman Empire could best be governed by Western nations and/or leaders they had specifically selected. In short order, the Middle East was divided: Palestine and Iraq were given to the British, Syria and Lebanon to the French. Even more disturbing to Abdul Aziz was that the remaining land was divided among members of Sharif Hussein's family. The sharif himself was proclaimed king of the Hijaz. His son Faisal was proclaimed king of Mesopotamia, which was renamed Iraq, and reported to Great Britain. The land that separated Iraq, Syria, and Palestine was labeled "Transjordan," and was handed over to another of King Hussein's sons,

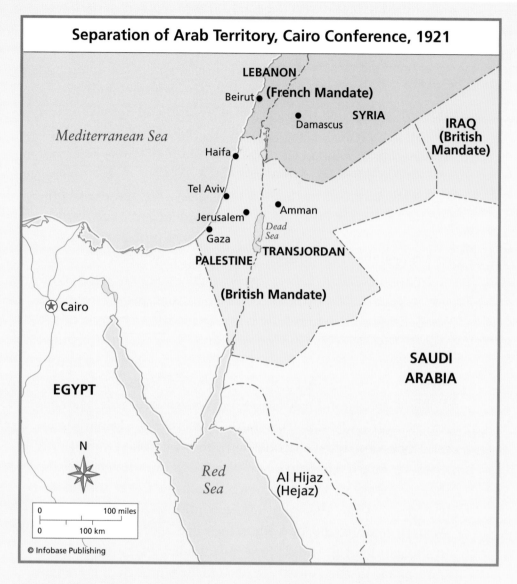

## Separation of Arab Territory, Cairo Conference, 1921

LEBANON
(French Mandate)
Beirut
SYRIA
Damascus
IRAQ (British Mandate)
Mediterranean Sea
Haifa
Tel Aviv
Jerusalem
Amman
Dead Sea
Gaza
TRANSJORDAN
PALESTINE
(British Mandate)
Cairo
SAUDI ARABIA
EGYPT
N
Red Sea
Al Hijaz (Hejaz)
0        100 miles
0        100 km
© Infobase Publishing

At a meeting in Cairo, Egypt, in March 1921, Winston Churchill presided over a conference that apportioned the Middle East. With the help of Gertrude Bell, T.E. Lawrence, and other foreign advisors, Churchill divided the region into separate countries, awarding bits and pieces of the Middle East to Sharif Hussein's family, while Abdul Aziz ruled over what is now Saudi Arabia.

Abdullah (partly to stop him from invading French-held Syria). He, too, would govern under an administration that reported to Great Britain.

So Abdul Aziz found himself ruling a portion of land bordered by countries that were led by members of Sharif Hussein's family—and all these unfriendly kingdoms were protected and advised by Great Britain. The time had come for a new meeting between Abdul Aziz and his old British contact, Percy Cox. The two met in the winter of 1922, in part to negotiate the boundaries that both sides would agree upon for the Saudi kingdom. But they were joined by an uninvited guest, a man from New Zealand named Frank Holmes, who initially claimed to be a butterfly hunter seeking a rare variety of black butterfly in the oasis of Qatif. Holmes was indeed from New Zealand, and he was looking for something rare and black in Qatif, but it was not butterflies. It was oil.

## LOST OPPORTUNITIES

When Cox learned of the arrival of the New Zealander, and his real motive, he demonstrated little interest in any meeting with the prospector. Claiming that he and Abdul Aziz were engaged in the far more important matter of settling boundaries, he tried to discourage Holmes from looking for oil.

Cox was not ignorant of the potential economic windfall the territory might offer from oil revenues. In fact, quite the opposite. Much of the Middle East had been taken by the British precisely because of its rich oil deposits, and although oil had yet to be discovered in Arabia, the British had already received hints that some might be found. They had little interest in seeing a non-British contractor move in. Cox went so far as to draft a letter to Holmes, indicating that he would not authorize his plan to look for oil in central Arabia without the approval of the British government. Then he gave the letter to Abdul Aziz and asked him to sign it.

Abdul Aziz was annoyed, but he did not want to lose the annuity he was receiving from the British government. He finally agreed to sign the letter, and Frank Holmes left.

But Holmes would be back. A year later, the British government announced that it was ending its policy of giving Arab leaders annual payments. Holmes did not waste any time. Quickly slipping into Arabia, he rushed to Abdul Aziz and presented his own financial offer in exchange for the right to prospect in Arabia. Abdul Aziz agreed.

But the story did not end there. Holmes's group, the Eastern and General Syndicate, did not invest much effort or money in trying to find oil in Arabia. Rather, the EGS believed that a much richer source of oil could be found in Bahrain, so that is where they invested most of their effort. Their investment paid off in 1932, when oil was struck in Bahrain.

The EGS stopped its payments to Abdul Aziz in 1927 and forfeited their rights to oil in Arabia. Little did they realize that they had given up the chance to find what would be the largest and richest source of oil in the world.

These annual payments would determine the course of Arabia's modern history. The Eastern and General's decision to stop its payments opened the door to American oil prospectors in the 1930s. Their discovery of oil would propel the Saudi family to an almost unimaginable fortune and would spark a relationship between the United States and Saudi Arabia that would drastically affect the politics of both countries.

And the decision by the British to stop their payments to Arab leaders—both to Abdul Aziz and Sharif Hussein—removed the one barrier that had kept the Saudis from attacking the Hijaz. Abdul Aziz had been dependent on British money to keep his kingdom financially stable, and the threat of its loss (should he attack a British ally) had kept him from challenging the agreed-upon boundaries. But now the money was gone, and Abdul Aziz needed another source of income. There was one source of steady, annual income in Arabia: the money that came from the international pilgrims who traveled each year to Mecca. The holy city that was located southwest of Riyadh garnered vast sums of money each year in fees and food and lodging.

Abdul Aziz had two choices: preside over a Saudi kingdom whose future was uncertain or launch an attack on Sharif Hussein. It did not take him long to decide which option to pursue.

# 5

# Birth of a Nation

As Abdul Aziz was planning his attack on the Hijaz, Sharif Hussein was focusing on a very different concern—the unexpected loss of British financial support. It was not only the loss of the annual payment that had proved disturbing; it was the clear signs that the British Empire was growing ever more distant.

The fault was in part that of the British, whose intelligence had led them to believe that Sharif Hussein's forces were vastly superior to any other army in the region. But the swift and bloody triumph by the Ikhwan at Kurmah had made it clear that their assumptions were flawed.

Worse, Sharif Hussein was becoming a very difficult and demanding ally. During the beginning of their alliance, the British had given him reason to believe that he would one day become king of all Arabs—a title that he assumed would give him the power to rule over all of Arabia, Iraq, Syria, Lebanon, and Palestine. Of course, the British never intended to give control of such a vast territory to one man, and while they had set up his sons in positions of power in the region, each country was kept separate and very firmly under British control.

At 71, Sharif Hussein was becoming bitter and angry about the way he thought the British had duped him. He grew moody and would often react violently, throwing anyone who displeased him into prison.

The loss of the British annual payment meant that he, too, began to search for alternative forms of revenue. His solution: a series of taxes—a water tax, a stamp tax, an income tax—on his own citizens. He also increased the cost of the pilgrimage to Mecca and banned the use of any conveyance during the pilgrimage except the special camels owned by his own family.

As rumors of Sharif Hussein's instability—and his people's discontent—began to spread, the British increasingly sought a more reliable ally in the region, in part to protect their own interests in the surrounding countries. They knew that a revolt or instability in the Hijaz—especially given the importance of the pilgrimage to Muslims—could quickly spread to Iraq, to Transjordan, or to Palestine. Suddenly, the prospect of Abdul Aziz marching on the holy cities was no longer a prospect that might force the British to react. It might instead be a welcome alternative.

## THE FINAL STRAW

The end of the reign of Sharif Hussein was sparked by a change not in Arabia, or even Great Britain, but instead in Turkey. The former heart of the Ottoman Empire was now in the hands of a modernizing leader named Mustafa Kemal Atatürk, who had determined that one of the keys to breaking with its past was to transform Turkey into a secular (nonreligious) state. On May 3, 1924, Sharif Hussein learned that Atatürk had decided to abolish the caliphate—the religious leadership of Islam that had been part of the Ottoman Empire for about 400 years. There would be no more caliph in Turkey, and this symbol of the faith was no longer based in Constantinople.

The symbolic leadership of Islam was there for the taking, and Sharif Hussein wasted no time in claiming it. On March 5, 1924, Sharif Hussein announced that, as guardian of the holy cities of Mecca and Medina, he would be the next caliph, the official successor to the Prophet Muhammad.

Within Hussein's kingdom, the news sparked little reaction. But the announcement made a much greater impression elsewhere. Muslims in other parts of the world suspected a British plot. Under British rule, India and Egypt were especially loyal to the Ottoman caliph (who had not ruled over them). The British,

Mustafa Kemal Atatürk *(above, center)* transformed Turkey into a secular state and did away with the caliph, a position representing the international Muslim community. Conferences were held to discuss the necessity of the caliphate (Cairo and Mecca, 1926; Jerusalem,1931) but Muslim nations failed to come to a consensus. Using his rule over the holy cities Mecca and Medina to legitimize his right to the title, Sharif Hussein declared that he was the next caliph.

in turn, expressed their dismay and announced that they would not recognize Hussein's new title. And in the Saudi kingdom, the news sparked great anger—anger that would be turned into opportunity.

## CONQUEST OF MECCA

Abdul Aziz understood the opportunity, but he was also well aware of the risks. The conquest of the Hijaz, particularly Mecca and Medina, would drastically change the Saudi Empire. For a devout Muslim such as Abdul Aziz, assuming control of the holy cities would mean a very different kind of responsibility than the one he held before. He was comfortable dealing with the Bedouins and overseeing an empire of desert and small settlements. But could he control a more urban community? Did he wish to extend the Saudi Empire into Mecca and Medina and take on the mantle of "guardian of the faith," which he would be required to do?

As before, Abdul Aziz did not want to be perceived as the conqueror of Mecca or Medina but rather as a welcomed guest. And so he called for a gathering of the ulama and other leaders in his kingdom and also sent out messengers to invite Muslims throughout the world. Abdul Aziz detailed for these leaders the problem posed by Sharif Hussein and requested that the international community of Muslims support a Wahhabi campaign to march into Mecca and force the sharif to step down.

There was little response to this message from the Saudis, but one of the few individuals who did respond made a critical difference. A representative from the Muslim population of India sent a note in support of the campaign. At the time, India was still a part of the British Empire. So, with this simple message, the British were influenced not to interfere with any attempt to march on the Hijaz. And so, with this final obstacle firmly removed, the Wahhabis prepared for war.

In August 1924, three months after the annual pilgrimage had ended, 3,000 Ikhwan soldiers began their march west toward the town of Taif. Sharif Hussein had been expecting the attack, and Taif's city walls had been fortified and equipped with guards and weapons. But when the Wahhabi warriors arrived, they found little resistance and within three days the city prepared to surrender.

It is not certain what happened next. Some argue that the residents of Taif did not clearly surrender and that one side fired upon another. All that is known is that the city's gates were opened to the Wahhabis and a massacre ensued. Everything of value was taken from the helpless citizens, and they were brutally slaughtered. As the army prepared to march on to Mecca, panic began to break out among the citizens there, who had heard rumors of the terrible events in Taif. Sharif Hussein pleaded for British assistance, but his request was denied.

The only possible hope lay in the immediate abdication of Sharif Hussein in favor of his son Ali, who might be able to negotiate a better deal with the Saudi forces. Surprisingly, Sharif Hussein agreed, perhaps knowing that without British support he had little hope of withstanding the assault. On the evening of October 3, 1924, he signed his letter of abdication. Within two weeks, the man who had claimed to be king of all Arabs, who had seized the caliphate and declared himself Muhammad's successor, was fleeing for his life. Granted, his flight was made somewhat easier by what he carried with him—several kerosene cans stuffed with hundreds of thousands of dollars in gold coins.

On the same day that Sharif Hussein left Arabia, four members of the Ikhwan army appeared outside the gates of Mecca. The gates were open, but everything else in town was closed—all of the shops and all of the windows and doors were shut and barred. Almost no one was in Mecca. The news of the massacre at Taif had frightened the citizens of Mecca so much that they had closed up their city and left, fleeing into the desert, into nearby cities, wherever they could go to escape the dreaded Ikhwan.

But Abdul Aziz had given strict instructions to his warriors: The holy city must not be damaged. And so the four Ikhwan who entered the city had dressed themselves in simple white clothes—the traditional garment worn by travelers who came to make the annual pilgrimage—and they had left their weapons behind. They were as defenseless as Mecca itself when they rode into the empty city to declare that it was now part of the Saudi Empire.

It would be three long months before Abdul Aziz arrived at Mecca to claim the city, and when he finally arrived, in December 1924, he made it clear that a new era had come. He refused to stay in the impressive palace Sharif Hussein had built; instead, he set up camp outside the city walls, took off his robes, and then he, too, put on the simple white clothes worn by all pilgrims.

With Mecca firmly in his control, Abdul Aziz turned to the other critical parts of the Hijaz: Medina and Jeddah. The siege of these two cities lasted for several months, in part because Abdul Aziz had given instructions to his Ikhwan forces not to utterly destroy the cities but to demand surrender. On the other side, Sharif Hussein's son Ali, who had inherited what remained of the kingdom, was left to defend the cities in a desperate last stand.

By December 1925, the last stand had come to an end. Ali left Jeddah, having been promised that he and his family could depart in peace to join his brother Faisal in Iraq and that his citizens would not be subjected to violence from the Ikhwan forces outside the city gates. Both promises were made, and the last remnants of the Hijaz became part of the Saudi Empire.

On January 8, 1926, Abdul Aziz was proclaimed the new king of the Hijaz by the leader of Mecca's holy mosque, al-Haram. He had taken back the last piece of the Saudi Empire, 24 years after his first victory in Riyadh had marked the beginning of the new age of Saudi leadership in Arabia.

## THE FINAL BATTLE

Abdul Aziz had succeeded in winning for himself the kingdoms of Najd (central Arabia) and the Hijaz. His victory had, in large part, been due to the fearsome fighting of the Ikhwan. The religious fervor that had inspired their willingness to fight to the death had expanded Abdul Aziz's territory. But as so often happens, the fervor also proved difficult to rein in once the need for battle had (in Abdul Aziz's eyes) been eliminated.

The Ikhwan turned their attention toward Iraq and other territories, and saw new lands to conquer and new people to convert. Abdul Aziz was satisfied with the size of his kingdom and had no wish to spark an international conflict on the basis of religious motives. So he faced a new challenge—convincing his fighting force to abandon the principles and the lifestyle that had guided them thus far. Instead, they should assume a more settled existence, one in which Saudi Arabia could begin the process of modernization.

The Ikhwan could not change their way of life. And so, once more, Abdul Aziz had to prepare to fight, but this time against some of the very men who had fought so fiercely on his side only a short time ago. For the first time, the Ikhwan would lose.

Two events shaped the course of the development of Saudi Arabia during the early part of the 1930s. Early in 1930, Abdul Aziz arranged a meeting with the ruler of Iraq, King Faisal, the son of his former enemy Sharif Hussein. Abdul Aziz made it clear, through their public and seemingly friendly encounters, that the era of conflict between the Saudis and members of Faisal's family (known as the Hashimites) had come to an end. Abdul Aziz's focus would no longer be on extending his empire but on governing it.

The second significant act took place in September 1932, when Abdul Aziz made the announcement that his two kingdoms—the kingdoms of Najd and Hijaz—would be unified and governed as a single land. The new kingdom would be known as Saudi Arabia. Its flag is green featuring a white sword and an Arabic inscription, the *shahadah* (the Islamic declaration of faith: There is no God but Allah, and Muhammad is his Messenger). The sha- hadah is considered holy and does not appear on T-shirts or other items. The flag is never flown at half-staff (a sign of mourning).

With this act, Abdul Aziz's campaign to restore the glory of the Saud name had finally succeeded. His new country—Saudi Arabia—extended over a territory as vast as that of western

A green flag with the shahadah has been linked to the Saud family since the eighteenth century. The sword was added to the flag in 1902 when Abdul Aziz became king of the Najd. Although there have been variations to the flag, its basic characteristics have been maintained. *Above*, a Saudi soldier holds the national flag in a parade before the beginning of the hajj in Mecca.

Europe. In little more than 30 years, he had created a kingdom that would become one of the most economically powerful nations in the world, all because of a precious commodity that lay below the sand.

## AMERICAN ENTERPRISE

As the 1930s unfolded, Abdul Aziz found himself the ruler of a vast kingdom, but one that was in need of money. Abdul Aziz had a reputation for generosity—anyone who visited his home at mealtimes was fed, and gifts were bestowed liberally and lavishly on those who were in need. It was in keeping with the Bedouin custom to share freely what one had, but this policy of giving often and generously had left the Saudi Empire impoverished.

It was for this reason that an American philanthropist named Charles R. Crane arrived in the kingdom. Crane came from a wealthy family, and he had served as an adviser to President Woodrow Wilson. He was familiar with the Middle East and, more significantly, in the past, he had proved his generosity to rulers of Middle Eastern countries.

Crane offered to provide the Saudis with a mining engineer who worked for him, a man named Karl Twitchell. And so, in the early part of 1931, Abdul Aziz was not thinking about oil, which Frank Holmes had failed to find nearly 10 years earlier. Instead, he was thinking of something that held far greater value for his people—water. Twitchell was hired to help find a water supply for the city of Jeddah.

After several weeks of travel through the Hijaz, Twitchell returned to Abdul Aziz with discouraging news. He had studied the land carefully, and there were no water resources there. But Abdul Aziz was desperate for potential sources of income and asked Twitchell to keep looking, in the hope that some other minerals might be found. Twitchell returned to the United States, looking for funding from an oil company that might be willing to support a more extensive exploration of Saudi Arabia's resources, because the kingdom itself had no money to under-write that expense. Unfortunately, no oil company was willing to back Twitchell's project.

Until that point, Abdul Aziz had little interest in oil or its potential revenues. But he soon learned that two neighboring rulers—the sheikhs of Bahrain and Kuwait—were receiving substantial sums of money for the rights to dig for oil in their tiny countries. Surely there must be some company, somewhere, that would pay him for the right to look for oil in Saudi Arabia. He went to Twitchell for advice, and the American gave him some valuable counsel. Twitchell told him to be patient and to wait to see if oil was found.

The answer came in June 1932. Oil was discovered in Bahrain, by the Standard Oil Company of California (Socal). With that discovery, it seemed very likely that oil also might be found in the Al-Hasa region of Saudi Arabia, only 25 miles away. Socal came to Abdul Aziz, offering to negotiate through one of his trusted advisers, Harry St. John Philby, while the Iraq Petroleum Company, a consortium owned jointly by British, French, American, and Dutch interests, sent its own British representative to plead its case. Abdul Aziz ultimately chose Socal, and an agreement was reached granting the company the right to search for oil in exchange for a substantial sum of money. Further details specified the amount the company would pay should oil be discovered and the amount that would be paid for the oil that was drilled. To Abdul Aziz, it was money for nothing. He had been told before that oil might be found beneath the sand, and nothing had been discovered. He was not confident that rumors of oil would be substantiated this time, but the money would help to sustain his kingdom.

At the time the Middle East was first partitioned, the British had expected to find oil, and the choice of lands to place under mandate was motivated by this knowledge. The desire for oil shaped many of the strategic decisions made by British politicians in the days after World War I. In Iraq, Kuwait, and Bahrain the British had been able to profit from their presence and from the willingness of local rulers to grant them the necessary prospecting concessions. But they did not realize the potential of Saudi Arabia until it was too late. In Saudi Arabia, it was the Saudis—and the Americans—who would benefit the most from their mistake.

## BLACK GOLD

In 1933, Socal set up its base and began the search for oil. For several years only small traces were found—nothing to support the hope of any major discovery. At one point, Abdul Aziz even asked the engineers to dig a few water wells, making it clear that he held far greater hope for the discovery of a source of water than of oil.

As the prospectors searched for oil, Abdul Aziz searched for a sensible solution to the question that had been troubling him for some time: Who would succeed him as ruler of Saudi Arabia? His oldest son, Turki, had died from influenza in 1919. His second son, Saud Ibn Abdul Aziz, was a gregarious and generous man, but he was not likely to be as capable as Abdul Aziz himself. As Abdul Aziz well knew, it had taken him a lifetime to develop the skills to meet so many competing needs and hold together such a vast kingdom. So, by the 1930s, he had decided upon a novel solution: The kingdom would be ruled by a committee or consensus, with both Saud and his brother Faisal ruling together, as king and crown prince. By passing the succession from brother to brother, rather than father to son, it was hoped that the family as a whole would gather together to choose the best leader. It would eliminate the possibility that a rivalry might arise should only one son be selected, who would then retain the power for his family alone.

It is this system that governed Saudi Arabia into the twenty-first century. The crown prince holds a position nearly as powerful as that of the king and also serves as an official spokesperson for the royal family. Major decisions are made by a contingent of family leaders. The king and crown prince are selected from those family members deemed best able to lead the country—a choice made with the knowledge that the wealth and power of all the family must be entrusted in the safest and most skillful hands. (In 2006, King Abdullah took steps to change this order of succession to avoid infighting in the next generation of Saudi princes.)

With the plan of succession resolved, next came a discovery that would make the entire family very rich. On March 20, 1938, the five-year quest of Socal, which had by this time assigned the project to its subsidiary, the California-Arabian Standard Oil Company (Casoc), ended. Seven wells had been dug into the rocky soil of Dammam Dome, in eastern Saudi Arabia, but they had yielded little. Finally, in desperation, a decision was made to extend the seventh well just a bit deeper. One mile below the earth's surface came the oil that would change nearly everything in Saudi Arabia—oil in seemingly endless supply, oil that would make Saudi Arabia one of the most economically powerful nations in the world, oil that would make the family of Abdul Aziz rich beyond anyone's imagination.

## THE WAGES OF WAR

The discovery of oil made Abdul Aziz a more important ally, but this brief period of diplomatic significance would be dimmed by the outbreak of World War II. Oil production ground to a halt, the trip across the Persian Gulf became a hazardous journey, and many of the oil workers returned to their homes.

Abdul Aziz spent the war astutely courting and being courted by both the Allies and Axis Powers. He concluded arms deals with both Germany and Italy, yet also maintained a strong relationship with the British. Neither side realized that he was negotiating with the other until well after the war had ended. By then Abdul Aziz had made clear that his sympathies had firmly been with the victorious Allied forces. But these sympathies would fade when it became clear that Great Britain once more intended

During a historic meeting between Abdul Aziz *(center)* and President Franklin D. Roosevelt *(right)*, the two discussed the future of Palestine and the placement of Jewish refugees from Europe. After his meeting, President Roosevelt sent Aziz a letter, stating, "I will take no action which might prove hostile to the Arab people." Roosevelt's promise was soon forgotten after his death in office.

to shape politics in the Middle East, this time by establishing a Jewish homeland in Arab-held Palestine.

By now, the United States had firmly entered the picture. An oil shortage in 1943 had illustrated how important it was for the United States to have access to the Saudi oil supply once the war came to an end. So Abdul Aziz was approached in confidence and asked if he would be willing to meet with President Franklin Roosevelt. He agreed.

On February 14, 1945, at the Great Bitter Lake in Egypt's Suez Canal, President Roosevelt welcomed the Saudi king on board the USS *Quincy*. On the agenda: the question of Palestine and ways to resolve what both sides felt was British mishandling of the problem.

After Roosevelt had outlined the tales of suffering the Jews had experienced, Abdul Aziz offered a simple and straightforward solution: The Jews should be given their choice of the best land and most impressive homes of the Germans who had been responsible for their suffering. The conversation moved on to other matters, and in the end, Abdul Aziz believed that Roosevelt had offered his assurance that the United States would not act in a manner hostile to the Arabs in regard to the Palestine question.

His meeting with British prime minister Winston Churchill, three days later, was less successful. Churchill ignored the Saudi prohibition on smoking and alcohol and consumed both in front of the Saudi king. Further, he had no interest in compromising on the question of the establishment of a Jewish state in Palestine. Instead he requested Abdul Aziz's support for the plan, in recognition of the support and friendship Great Britain had offered throughout the years.

Apparently, Churchill had mixed up the facts—in reality, Great Britain had offered little support to Abdul Aziz and instead had consistently supported his rival. But Abdul Aziz returned home confident in the promises Roosevelt had offered—that Palestinian Arabs would be protected and involved in any decisions regarding the settlement of Palestine.

But the promises made by Roosevelt would soon be forgotten, because by April 1945 he was dead and the new president, Harry S. Truman, indicated a willingness to support the establishment of a Jewish homeland in Palestine.

# 6

# Death of a Nation Builder

The story of the creation of modern Saudi Arabia begins with Abdul Aziz, but it does not end there. For the history of this important part of the Middle East extends beyond the life and achievements of one man and reflects the attitudes and actions of his family as well.

By 1953, Abdul Aziz was nearly 77 years old. He was suffering from arthritis so severe that it had left him crippled and confined to a wheelchair, and he had become nearly blind. A powerful nation had been created, but the man who had made it happen was finding it increasingly difficult to govern it.

On November 9, 1953, Abdul Aziz died, having overseen the restoration of his family's power and honor. In keeping with Islamic traditions as understood by the Wahhabis, the man who had established Saudi Arabia was buried in an unmarked grave in Riyadh. There is no headstone or any sign to mark the final resting place of the man who so drastically altered the history of his homeland.

The story of the son who inherited the Saudi throne illustrates the best and worst of the kingdom Abdul Aziz had built. In a sense, the new king, Saud, was in an impossible position—compared either with the dynamic leader his father had been or with the tireless and intelligent manager his brother Faisal would later become. At the beginning of his reign, King Saud constructed a multimillion-dollar palace, complete with swimming pools and mosques. Eleven years later, as his reign was ending in chaos and disarray, he would choose to end his time as king barricaded within those same walls.

Many of King Saud's accomplishments are overlooked because of the corruption and financial mismanagement that characterized his reign. However, he was instrumental in strengthening Islam within the kingdom. He decided to abolish the annual tax that Muslim pilgrims had traditionally paid for the privilege of visiting Mecca, saying that he could afford to pay the tax for them.

In fact, a generous nature was one of the few traits that King Saud inherited from his father. He gave liberally to Islamic causes, helped to create welfare facilities, and gave money for hospitals, schools, and new highways. It was not long before King Saud had successfully managed to nearly bankrupt the kingdom with his programs, facilities, and government offices, all designed to better his people's lives but all terribly expensive to maintain.

The second in line to the throne, Crown Prince Faisal, was the exact opposite of his brother, the king. Saud was tall; Faisal was short and thin. Saud had a large family, with many wives; Prince Faisal had one wife and a small family. King Saud was generous and unwilling to see the difference between the country's income and his own; Prince Faisal was more modest in his expenses and possessions.

Despite, or perhaps because of, these differences, King Saud was a popular king and deemed the best choice to succeed his father. The people appreciated his support of Islamic causes and his generous giving toward programs that would benefit the citizens of Saudi Arabia.

But early in his regime, King Saud demonstrated a weakness in two critical areas: business and diplomacy. An attempted oil-shipping deal with the wealthy Greek tycoon Aristotle Onassis drew intense protests from the U.S. oil companies that would be expected to pay for the privilege of using someone else's ships instead of their own. The Americans also feared that, once the Saudis had begun the process of controlling the oil tankers, they might soon move to take control of the oil fields themselves. Their threatened withdrawal from Saudi Arabia was enough to make King Saud change his mind—the kingdom would not fare well without the critical influx of money the oil fields provided. The deal fell apart, but soon other areas of the kingdom began to fall apart as well.

The king had grown tired of being lectured by his brother Faisal and other members of his family. Gradually, he fired the Council of Ministers who had been created under Abdul Aziz. He found more worthwhile advice from his own sons and his friends; essentially those who would shower him with compliments rather than complaints.

The transition in leadership that had first seemed orderly began to become fractious at a particularly dangerous time. Throughout the Middle East, Arabs who were dissatisfied by the corrupt regimes ruling them were being drawn to the charismatic colonel Gamal Abdel Nasser, who had helped engineer the overthrow of the Egyptian monarchy in 1952. Nasser's message was that the Arab people had been artificially divided, by barriers created first by the Ottomans and later by the British and other Western powers. Nasser preached that the Arabs really were one nation and should be united under a single government—a government that, not coincidentally, he planned to lead.

Viewing Egypt as an ally, King Saud agreed to Nasser's request that they become partners in this new venture to unify Arabs everywhere. He agreed to help underwrite the cost of Arab newspapers publishing Nasser's message throughout the Middle East. He was also happy to welcome the arrival of Egyptian soldiers who would, he was promised, help shape the Saudi army into a more modern fighting force, and Egyptian teachers who came to help staff the new schools King Saud was building. These teachers and soldiers had little understanding of the more traditional Arabian society. Instead, their message drew Saud's subjects' attention to the growing gap between the many wealthy members of the Saudi family (who continued to increase in numbers and income) and the rest of Arabian society.

King Saud had alienated the Americans once by his proposal to negotiate an oil tanker deal with Onassis. Now, his alliance with Nasser posed another threat to Western interests. It was Saudi money that was enabling Nasser to spread his message of Arab unity throughout the Middle East, and Saudi money, some

Despite a positive alliance, the partnership between Egyptian president Gamal Nasser and King Saud soon soured after the monarch traveled to the United States. King Saud's determination to improve his country's relationship with the pro-Israel U.S. government caused other Middle Eastern nations to turn against him. *Above*, anchored ships in the Suez Canal in Egypt, a key factor in the Arab-Israeli conflict.

suspected, that also helped finance an Egyptian arms deal with the USSR.

The trouble became more serious in July 1956, when Egypt nationalized the Suez Canal. The canal was a critical waterway, both for oil shipments and other supplies, and the move angered the British, French, and Israelis. When war followed, King Saud had little choice but to agree to allow Egyptian planes to use his airfields and to cut off oil sales to Great Britain and France. But he was not pleased that a move that would so seriously jeopardize his country's economy was not discussed with him first.

An answer to the problem soon came, in the offer of a stronger partnership from the United States. King Saud agreed to travel to the United States to meet President Dwight Eisenhower. The United States wanted the right to continue to use Dhahran Airport for an air force post; King Saud wanted more economic and military aid. He received both, plus a new role in the so-called "Eisenhower Doctrine"—the king was to act as a moderating force among other Arab nations, a move that would put him in competition with Nasser as an Arab leader.

Nasser wasted no time in turning on his former ally. Egypt's government-controlled radio stations issued daily bulletins outlining the excesses and real or imagined corruption of the Saudi royal family and called upon all Arabs to overthrow the regime.

## BROTHER TO BROTHER

The growing threat to the Saudi kingdom alarmed the second in line to the throne, Crown Prince Faisal. Faisal had found himself gradually being eased out of any kind of decision-making role. He had been appointed president of the Council of Ministers, but Saud seldom consulted the council over any important matters.

In fact, Saud had recently promoted several of his sons to important positions within the government, bypassing more senior and better-qualified members of the family. Faisal and others in the family were also concerned that this promotion of Saud's sons meant that he planned to ignore their father's plan of succession for the throne; that rather than seeing the kingship pass from brother to brother, Saud intended to hand power to one of his sons.

Of equal concern were the constant changes in foreign policy. The alliance and then breakdown of the relationship with Nasser had served little except to prompt the Egyptian leader to call for the overthrow of the Saudi monarchy, a call that had a willing audience among many Saudi citizens dismayed at their king's excessive spending. Saud was even outspending the vast sums pouring in from oil revenues, and the country was teetering on the brink of bankruptcy.

By March 1958, many of the brothers of the House of Saud were meeting secretly to work out a solution to the troubles facing the kingdom. On March 22, they met with King Saud and offered the only possible answer. He could remain king, but the day-to-day management of the kingdom must be handed over to Crown Prince Faisal. To everyone's surprise, he agreed.

It was the system that Abdul Aziz had loosely defined when he first began to plan for his succession—a system where the strengths and weaknesses of the two brothers could complement, rather than frustrate, each other's actions. Faisal's first action involved establishing control over government spending. He cut back on all but the most critical expenses and also severely limited the extra money that had been available to members of the royal family, over and above their fixed annual allowances.

Faisal's personal example helped make the new cutbacks more acceptable to all. He had no entourage and no bodyguards, and he frequently drove his own car rather than use a chauffeur. He worked long hours and kept a simple home in stark contrast to the more lavish palaces of other members of the royal family.

More than anything else, he was always prepared. In August 1960, the CEO of the world's largest oil company at the time, Standard Oil of New Jersey, announced that they needed to cut their prices. As a result, they would be paying less for the oil they purchased from Saudi Arabia. Crown Prince Faisal was angry but ready for the drop in revenues. The price cut would mean a loss of millions of dollars from his carefully prepared budget, at a time when he was beginning to see some improvements in his country's economic status.

But Faisal had a plan—a plan for a union of oil-producing countries that would be able to stand up to the major oil

When it became clear King Saud was incapable of managing Saudi Arabia, power was quickly transferred to his brother, Crown Prince Faisal *(above center)*. After establishing a new national budget, Faisal soon helped form OPEC, a group of representatives from oil-producing countries.

companies. On September 9, 1960, five countries—Saudi Arabia, Iraq, Iran, Venezuela, and Kuwait—came together in Iraq to plan a new strategy. The new organization they formed would be known as the Organization of the Petroleum Exporting Countries, or OPEC. Other countries would join OPEC over the years, but at the beginning it was these five nations that took a stand to ensure greater involvement in determining market prices for their countries' valuable resource.

Key to the success of OPEC was the pledge of unity—that no nation would cut a separate deal with an oil company if it would damage one of the other members of the organization. With this action, oil suddenly became more than a resource—it became a political tool, an asset that could be used to shift the balance of power away from the West and toward the members of OPEC.

It was a victory for Arab unity and a personal triumph for Faisal. Unfortunately, he had enjoyed a few too many triumphs since assuming a more active role in Saudi affairs—balancing the budget, creating economic stability, and now overseeing the establishment of a new international entity. King Saud had tired of his ceremonial role and the focus on his brother's accomplishments. In December 1960, he announced that he was reclaiming the full powers of the kingship and also naming himself president of the Council of Ministers.

The move was generally supported by family members who had been forced to make their own cutbacks under Faisal's campaign of frugality. Some of them had felt that Faisal had not paid sufficient attention to their needs; others felt that he had gone too far with his cutbacks.

But within a year, King Saud fell gravely ill. Doctors within Saudi Arabia were unable to care for him properly, so it was decided that the only possibility of a cure required him to seek care outside the country. Less than a year after he was unceremoniously demoted, Faisal was back in power.

## AN OLD FOE

By mid-August 1962, Nasser had renewed his call for Arabs to overthrow the Saudi family, indicating that Arab attempts to free Jerusalem from the Israelis should be preceded by the liberation of Riyadh. One month later, a revolution in neighboring Yemen had ousted the royal family there, and Egyptian forces arrived to help form a revolutionary government and then make plans to carry the revolution north into Saudi Arabia.

These developments were particularly troubling to Crown Prince Faisal, who was once more in the number-two spot. King Saud had returned from medical treatments a few months earlier and had, once more, taken back full power. But the events in Yemen, so close to the Saudi border, were deemed enough of an emergency to prompt the family to insist that Faisal should again be involved in day-to-day operations, in part to plan a strategy for the possibility of war.

Faisal quickly cemented an informal alliance with President John F. Kennedy. The United States would provide military support by arranging joint military exercises. In exchange, Faisal agreed to institute certain reforms in Saudi Arabia—including the abolition of slavery. This was carried out by the government itself, which paid for the freedom of all slaves in the kingdom.

It had been a small price to pay for what would prove sufficient military power to repel an Egyptian attack. Nasser's forces had superior weapons (courtesy of arms trading with the USSR), but soon U.S. jet fighters were flying over Riyadh and Jeddah, a clear signal that an Egyptian attack would meet not only with Saudi, but also U.S., resistance.

The threat to Saudi Arabia from an outside force was thus successfully averted, but the internal struggles within the royal family were much more difficult to manage. King Saud simply did not wish to be a king in name only. He began to seek support from outsiders when he found the ranks of his family closing against him. He turned to tribal sheikhs, the ulama, even those who were suspected of supporting Nasser. This was the final straw for his exasperated family; Saud had broken the family rule of never showing weakness to outsiders. As the family began to turn against him, Saud barricaded himself in his royal palace and surrounded it with members of the Saudi Royal Guard. In response, other brothers placed the armed forces on high alert, and the national guard was called up.

It was a tense time, finally resolved at the end of 1963, when King Saud came out of his palace and agreed to allow Faisal to remain in charge, provided that he be allowed to represent Saudi Arabia in the upcoming Arab conference in Cairo. Once more the brothers reached an agreement; once more King Saud ignored the agreement within a few months; and, by March 1964, Saud was once more demanding full control of the country.

But this time the outcome was very different. In the last dispute, it had been made clear that Faisal had the full support not only of his family but of the ulama as well. Now the ulama agreed to draw up a *fatwa* (a religious ruling) stating that Faisal's powers would be his permanently, and that Saud would serve only as the head of state and not the ruler.

King Saud was furious, refusing to accept his role as a figure-head. He insisted that the ulama and the family reconsider their decision. The leading members of the family and leading representatives of the ulama came together and found themselves in total agreement. There could not be a king of Saudi Arabia in name only. King Saud must abdicate, and Faisal must be declared the new king of Saudi Arabia. On November 3, 1964, King Saud agreed to step down and went into exile.

# 7

# The Diligent King

King Faisal had demonstrated that his governing approach was radically different from that of his brother. He focused on work, carving out a precise schedule of long hours, interrupted only by the call to prayer that marks life in Saudi Arabia five times a day.

His reign lasted from 1964 until 1975, during which time Faisal's discipline and diligence transformed palace life from indulgent excess to a focus on the family business—the family business being, of course, ruling Saudi Arabia. But it was definitely not business as usual under Faisal's leadership. In the same way that he had quietly and efficiently streamlined Saudi Arabia's economy as crown prince, his time as king was marked by additional domestic reforms, many of these influenced by his wife, Iffat. It was Iffat's focus on public education that helped transform what had been a restrictive system of schooling into more contemporary training for students. Iffat helped to oversee the introduction of more modern subjects into school studies—for example, science and foreign languages—and, perhaps most controversial of all, she helped champion the cause of education for girls. In a country where women live essentially separate lives, where they are not allowed to drive a car or appear in public unveiled, the concept of training them for more meaningful endeavors led to intense debate.

While his wife was helping to spark greater opportunities for women's education, Faisal was focusing on the unifying opportunities Islam presented. Faisal saw this as an important check to the revolutionary cries of nationalism championed by Nasser.

There was no need, in Faisal's eyes, to create yet another kind of unity for Arabs, one in which the unity offered by faithful devotion to the tenets of Islam provided an all-encompassing connection.

Faisal traveled to various countries in the Middle East, Asia, and Africa, calling upon Muslims to unite to form a force that

One of King Faisal's many national reforms is the modernization of the country's education system. Iffat, the king's wife, pushed for the study of science and foreign languages, as well as the inclusion of female students. *Above*, female students participate in a graphic design project at the Dar El-Hekma College for Women in Jeddah.

could wield tremendous international influence. The Six-Day War of 1967, in which Israel launched a preemptive attack on Syria, Jordan, and Egypt, was a bitter disappointment to King Faisal, resulting in Israel's capture of Jerusalem, a city holy to Muslims as well as to Jews and Christians. But it firmed his resolve that greater ties were needed among the Arab states, leading to a peacemaking gesture toward the defeated Egyptian president Nasser.

It also marked the beginning of a change in the relationship between Saudi Arabia and the United States. While Nasser had been an enemy, the United States had been a valuable ally. But now Nasser's threat had diminished, and the United States had become an enthusiastic supporter of Israel. In part, the support of Israel was viewed by U.S. policymakers as a countermove against the supply of Russian arms flowing into Egypt and Syria. But it was a vicious cycle, one that could be viewed quite differently depending on which side one was on. For the United States, support of Israel helped balance the growing Russian presence among the neighboring Arab nations. But as the United States supplied more arms to Israel, the Arab states negotiated their own arms deals to stave off the growing threat from Israel.

## CHANGING TIMES

By 1973, Anwar Sadat had been serving as Egypt's president for three years. He had attempted to resolve the growing tension between Egypt and Israel, but his tentative efforts at peacemaking had been ignored by President Richard Nixon, whose focus was on Vietnam and the growing conflict there. Sadat and King Faisal shared a conviction that the buildup in arms deliveries from the United States to Israel would inevitably lead to war.

King Faisal sent a signal to Washington, D.C.—a message carried by his oil minister to leading members of President Nixon's cabinet. It noted the need for the United States to moderate arms shipments to Israel or face the consequences. But it was a message that was largely dismissed as an empty threat.

On October 6, 1973, Egyptian troops crossed the Suez Canal to attack Israeli forces on the other side, while Syria concurrently invaded the Golan Heights, which Israel had taken in 1967. It was Yom Kippur, the Jewish Day of Atonement. As the war began to unfold, a meeting was held between members of OPEC and the oil companies. OPEC made it clear that it would raise oil prices for those nations that supported Israel in the war. By October 12, talks had broken down, with the oil companies requesting the right to consult their governments before agreeing to such a drastic rise in prices. Their opinion quickly became irrelevant. The OPEC nations met again on October 17, this time setting the price of oil themselves. It would mark a dramatic change in the way oil companies would do business with Arab nations from then on—with that decision, it became the right of the oil-producing countries, rather than the companies, to set the price of their oil.

King Faisal was not happy, but he did not want to cripple the United States. He decided that a small cutback in production was in order—just enough to send the message that the OPEC nations meant business. But President Nixon was determined to increase the amount of aid previously agreed upon for Israel, from $850 million to $2.2 billion.

It was a sum of money that would drastically turn the tide of the war in Israel's favor, but would prove an expensive decision, in more ways than one. On October 19, 1973, King Faisal received the news of the increase in funding for Israel. And on that day, he announced that all shipments of oil to the United States were to be immediately halted.

## A NEW POWER

The oil embargo had a drastic impact on life in the United States, other Western countries, and even Japan. Those who had underestimated the power of a Saudi king suddenly understood how dramatically dependence on oil had shifted the balance of global power. By 1974, a new round of diplomacy had brought an end to the embargo, with the promise of the delivery of U.S. tanks, naval ships, and fighter aircraft to Saudi Arabia.

Suddenly, investment was everywhere. The new price of oil had brought vast revenues to the country and presented it with a problem—how to spend all the money. There were plenty of businessmen eager to offer a solution, and soon cars and consumer goods were pouring into the country.

The money made many Saudis happy, but King Faisal was not one of them. He had taken certain steps not to become wealthy but out of a profound belief that he was doing the right thing. He did not like the way that this sudden rush of riches was transforming his country and its people. But he did not have long to worry about his country's new status.

On the morning of March 25, 1975, the king's 26-year-old nephew, Faisal ibn Musaed, walked into his uncle's palace and joined a delegation from Kuwait who had come to meet with the king. When they walked in, so did he, and as the king reached out to greet his nephew, the young man pulled out a pistol and fired it three times. King Faisal died soon afterwards.

No one really understood what had prompted the young man to assassinate his uncle. The truth seemed to be a collection of small details: The young man had been mentally unstable; he had been drinking the night before; his younger brother had been killed 10 years earlier and Faisal ibn Musaed felt the king had been responsible. There were few answers.

Many would remember the reign of King Faisal as the high point of the Saudi Empire. He had transformed Saudi life, while clinging to traditional values. He had made his nation an international power, yet preserved the influence and prestige of the monarchy at a time when Arab nations all around him were falling victim to Nasser's nationalist movement. He had held the kingdom together at its weakest moment and made it a power that was both respected and feared.

## A NEW ERA

King Faisal's death, while unexpected, did not plunge the monarchy into chaos. The system of succession had been firmly established, so the transfer of power was orderly. With the blessing of both the Saudi family and the ulama, Faisal's 63-year-old half brother, Khalid, became king, and his brother Fahd became crown prince.

The king who came to power in 1975 was a moderate who had little experience in politics. Contemporary observers expected that, because he was in poor health when he became king, he would only serve briefly. Initially it was felt that the two brothers—the more traditional Khalid and the more modern Fahd—would mirror the relationship of Saud and Faisal. But the truth proved subtler. The system by which the family governs, and the decisions about who will inherit the throne and who will be second and third in line, are considered by the family members and, in some sense, designed to provide checks and balances. Crown Prince Fahd was known for his pro-Western stance, but third in line to the throne was his brother Abdullah, who was known for his anti-American attitudes and support of Arab nationalist leaders. In this way, the Saudi family ensured that no one member could swing the country too far in one direction or the other.

But a system designed to check unlimited power can produce rifts and disagreements, and this is what began to emerge in the late 1970s. By 1977, much of the kingdom's economic problems had been solved by the influx of investments and money from the production of oil. The citizens were leading increasingly modern lifestyles—a fact that disturbed the ulama, who feared that the Saudi family was abandoning its Wahhabi principles and guiding the country in the wrong

The two brothers in line for the throne after King Faisal's death were princes Khalid *(right)* and Fahd *(left)*. Fahd was appointed Crown Prince and Khalid succeeded Faisal, but due to Khalid's health problems Fahd had authority over the daily operations of the kingdom. Once he became king in 1982, he was known for his close ties to Western governments, while also taking an active role in Middle East politics.

direction. King Khalid's health was a concern; it was clear that a new king would soon inherit the throne, and a split was developing between those who supported Prince Fahd's pro-Western stance and those who supported Prince Abdullah's more Arab-oriented views.

International events at the time illustrated the important gap between the two princes' positions. In early 1979, the monarchy of the Shah of Iran (a close ally of the United States) was overthrown by Shiite fundamentalists. This revolution sparked tremendous concern in Saudi Arabia. Then, in September 1978, the Camp David Accords between President Sadat of Egypt, U.S. president Jimmy Carter, and Prime Minister Menachem Begin of Israel led to renewed focus on the question of Palestine, particularly what the Saudi position would be. The pro-Western stance of Crown Prince Fahd was unpopular, and he faced the prospect of being overthrown if he became king. As a result, the Saudi family decided that it was a good time for Crown Prince Fahd to leave the country for a while. During this extended "vacation," Prince Abdullah and others changed the foreign policy of Saudi Arabia, choosing to loosen many of their diplomatic ties with the United States. Instead, they developed firmer links to other Arab nations, while condemning Egypt's treaty with Israel and raising oil prices.

To many, this change in foreign policy, the uncertainty generated by King Khalid's poor health, and the internal disagreement within the family meant that the Saudi monarchy was in its final days. A crisis in Mecca would further challenge the family's resolve and its position.

## THE MECCA REBELLION

On the night of November 19, 1979, a young man named Juhayman ibn Muhammad ibn Sayf al Utaybi entered the grounds of the Masjid al-Haram, or Grand Mosque, in Mecca—a shrine viewed by Muslims as the holiest place in the world. He was not alone. With him were nearly 500 followers, and they were equipped with supplies of food and an arsenal of weapons. Early the next morning—a date that marked the beginning of a new year in the Muslim calendar—they stormed the mosque, firing their rifles and shooting at anyone who blocked them from entering. They quickly seized control of the Grand Mosque and barricaded themselves inside.

The young man who led the rebellion and his followers were supporters of a kind of neo-Ikhwan philosophy. They believed that the Saudi family had led the country astray with its modernization and the rapid increase in wealth. They preached the need for a return to the traditional values, the old way of life, and believed that they had in their midst the new *Mahdi*, or "right-guided one," who would lead the country from its old, corrupt ways and instead focus on traditional teachings.

For the Saudi family, this event was a disaster. They had claimed for themselves the title of Protector of the Holy Places, so the seizure of the Grand Mosque proved that their claim was hollow. Police surrounded the temple, but King Khalid hesitated about how best to proceed. The Koran specifically prohibited any desecration of a mosque. Not only would it be a sin to kill a person there, but the Koran dictated that not even animals or plants could be destroyed within the holy grounds. For this reason, the army or police could not simply fight their way in and overpower Juhayman and his men.

King Khalid requested a meeting with the ulama and asked their permission for the government to shoot if necessary in order to win back the mosque. Permission was granted. But the Saudi army still needed to be careful to ensure that the mosque was not seriously damaged or, worse, destroyed. It took two weeks before the rebels finally surrendered and not before many people had died in attempting to retake the mosque.

The royal family's reputation was damaged by the ease at which Juhayman and his men seized the Grand Mosque

Inspired by the history of the Ikhwan and hostile to the Saudi government, Juhay-man al-Utaybi organized a group of about 1,000 to 1,500 followers and seized control of Mecca's Grand Mosque *(above)*. Pakistani and French security forces retook the shrine in a battle that left about 250 casualties and 600 wounded. Al-Utaybi and 63 of his surviving followers were later beheaded.

and by their inability to quickly suppress the revolt. While criticism was strong against the militants for their actions—shooting guns and killing people on holy ground—the group's denunciations of the royal family and their calls for a return to more conservative religious values touched a nerve. As a result, both King Khalid and Crown Prince Fahd began to delegate more authority to the ulama to oversee religious and moral aspects of life in Saudi Arabia and to ensure that the push to modernize did not lead to the abandonment of traditional Wahhabi ways.

## A STRUGGLE FOR POWER

King Khalid's reign ended with his death in June 1982 after a long series of illnesses. Crown Prince Fahd became the new king, and Prince Abdullah was named crown prince. Although the prearranged succession seemed to proceed smoothly, the differences that had distinguished Fahd and Abdullah grew more pronounced as they assumed the most senior positions in the kingdom. Abdullah still opposed the pro-Western tilt of the new king's policies. He also resented the fact that he, in the number-two position in the country, would have far less power than his brother had wielded when he had served as crown prince. During much of King Khalid's reign, his poor health had forced Fahd to take over the day-to-day administration of Saudi Arabia. Abdullah knew that his own position as crown prince would involve less authority.

Concerned by the rise of Islamic fundamentalist movements throughout the Arab world, Fahd underscored the importance of the ulama, whose position had been strengthened considerably by the siege of the Grand Mosque in Mecca. King Fahd met weekly with the religious leaders, consulting them to ensure that the pace of modernization did not radically undercut the Sharia, the Islamic law that is the basis for judicial decisions in Saudi Arabia.

These steps would win back some public support, but the regime was confronted by a new group of dissatisfied citizens—a growing middle class that was well educated and that had experienced prosperity. They had no wish to return to the days before oil, but they had become dissatisfied with a royal family that seemed to grow richer and more powerful at a time when jobs and opportunities were no longer plentiful for the rest of the country's citizens.

As the 1980s unfolded, there was a sense that the prosperity enjoyed by the people of Saudi Arabia, and its rulers, had perhaps come to an end. The question was, what would come next? Would Saudi Arabia choose to side with the Arab nations whose own monarchies had been overthrown by radical movements? Or would it choose to move closer to Western nations?

The choice became clearer in August 1990, when the leader of Iraq sent his troops into Kuwait and then turned his sights on Saudi Arabia.

# 8

# A Storm in the Desert

From 1980 until 1988, the countries of the Middle East had witnessed a bitter war between Iraq and Iran. Saudi Arabia, Kuwait, and several other nations (including the United States) had supported Iraqi leader Saddam Hussein's efforts to combat the revolutionary regime in Iran. But when the war finally ended, both the Saudi and Kuwaiti governments expected that the loans they had made to Iraq would be repaid. This enraged Saddam Hussein, who felt that he had helped combat the spread of Iran's brand of revolutionary Islam on behalf of all of the neighboring Middle Eastern countries and should not be expected to make any kind of repayment.

Saddam Hussein had little interest in repaying his debts at a time when the postwar Iraqi government was experiencing economic troubles. Ultimately he had a very different plan in mind. On August 2, 1990, an army of 100,000 Iraqi troops and 300 tanks rolled across the border into Kuwait. The Kuwaiti army, a mere 16,000 men, was no match for this invasion force. The Kuwaiti emir (the ruler of the tiny country) and his family fled their land, and the Kuwaiti armed forces quickly surrendered.

*(opposite)* After the Iraqi invasion of Kuwait, many were concerned that Saudi Arabia was Saddam Hussein's next target. Iraqi control of the Hama oil fields, one of Saudi Arabia's largest, in addition to Kuwait's and Iraq's reserves, would have given Hussein control over the majority of the world's reserves. The United States, looking to protect their source of oil, dispatched nearly 500,000 troops to Saudi Arabia for Operation Desert Storm.

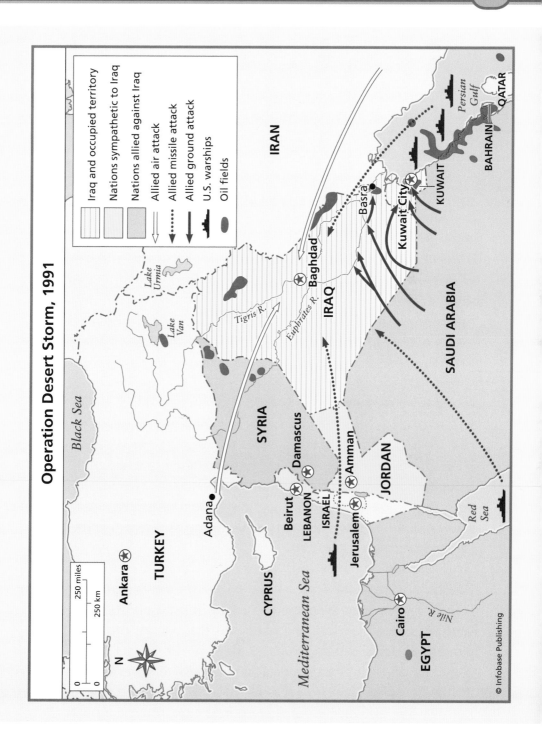

## Operation Desert Storm, 1991

**Legend:**
- Iraq and occupied territory
- Nations sympathetic to Iraq
- Nations allied against Iraq
- Allied air attack
- Allied missile attack
- Allied ground attack
- U.S. warships
- Oil fields

TURKEY
Ankara ✪
Adana ●

Black Sea

Lake Van
Lake Urmia

IRAN

SYRIA
Damascus ✪

Tigris R.
Euphrates R.

Baghdad ✪

IRAQ

Basra ●

Kuwait City ✪
KUWAIT

Persian Gulf
QATAR
BAHRAIN

SAUDI ARABIA

Beirut ✪
LEBANON
ISRAEL
Jerusalem ✪
Amman ✪
JORDAN

Mediterranean Sea

CYPRUS

Red Sea

Nile R.
Cairo ✪
EGYPT

N

250 miles
250 km
0

© Infobase Publishing

The invasion, and the clear indication that Saudi Arabia would be the next target of the Iraqi forces, prompted a swift reaction. At the heart of the U.S.-Saudi relationship had been a basic understanding—Saudi Arabia provided the oil, while the United States promised the security. With Iraqi troops marching across Kuwait toward Saudi Arabia, the time had come to focus on the "security" part of the relationship.

Within only a few months, some 500,000 U.S. soldiers were dispatched to Saudi Arabia in preparation for a military campaign that would be known as Operation Desert Storm. The agreement that led to this massive deployment of U.S. troops in the kingdom was not formalized; instead, it was the work of extensive and detailed diplomatic meetings. While the clear short-term goal was to force the Iraqis to withdraw from Kuwait (and ensure that they did not invade Saudi Arabia), the exact length of time for which U.S. troops would be deployed in Saudi Arabia was never specified. It was understood that they would remain for as long as it took—but this vague understanding would be cause for concern when several thousand U.S. soldiers still remained stationed on Saudi soil long after the military operation.

Part of the criticism was based in the religion that has guided so many Saudi political decisions. More conservative Muslims felt that it was a violation of their independence to have foreign soldiers permanently stationed in the country where two of their holiest shrines were located

The coalition forces quickly drove the Iraqi forces out of Kuwait. But while the Saudis were able to protect their country from invasion, they were less successful in their efforts to prevent an economic crisis. Oil prices fell throughout the 1990s, steadily reducing Saudi income. Deficits in the budget became common, and the Saudis' initial willingness to cover the cost of supporting U.S. troops in Saudi Arabia soon turned to reluctance, as the presence of foreign troops began to pose a public relations problem.

## NEW POLITICS FOR A NEW AGE

The years 1995 and 1996 were marked by twin attacks in Saudi Arabia, this time against American targets. Both were in locations heavily populated by U.S. soldiers. The first took place in Riyadh, and Saudi police quickly arrested four men who confessed to the bombing. They claimed that their actions had been inspired by Osama bin Laden, the son of a wealthy Saudi businessman with links to the royal family who had been

In hopes of intimidating U.S. troops into leaving Saudi Arabia, terrorists exploded a deadly truck bomb at Dhahran's Khobar Towers, a facility that provided housing for the U.S. military. The blast was felt 20 miles away in the Persian Gulf country of Bahrain. At least 19 people were killed and hundreds were injured.

preaching an anti-Western message from locations throughout central Asia, the Middle East, and even Africa. The men were swiftly beheaded.

The second attack took place in Dhahran, at the Khobar Towers, where many U.S. servicemen had been living. Again, it became clear that there was a connection to Saudi fundamentalists. In total, 24 Americans were killed in the two incidents, and the United States responded by relocating its personnel to a more remote location in the desert.

As the 1990s drew to a close, King Fahd's health began to fail. He had suffered a stroke in 1995. Crown Prince Abdullah stepped forward and began to handle the day-to-day management of the kingdom when Fahd was unable to oversee state affairs.

In 2003, responding both to security concerns and intense pressure from Saudi citizens, the United States announced that it would pull out almost all of its troops from Saudi Arabia, ending a 12-year military presence. Only one month after the announcement, suicide bombers killed 35 people at housing compounds for Westerners in Riyadh, hours before then-U.S. secretary of state Colin Powell arrived for a planned visit.

During this period, the Saudi people pressed for social reform. In September 2003, more than 300 Saudi intellectuals (male and female) signed a petition calling for political reforms. A rally was held in October in the center of Riyadh. Police were called in to break up the gathering and more than 270 people were arrested.

In November 2003, a suicide attack linked to al Qaeda militants targeted a residential compound in Riyadh. Many were injured in the attack, and 17 were killed. Responding to the pressure, Crown Prince Abdullah announced a decision to grant wider powers to the Saudi Consultative Council (*majlis al-shura*), including a provision that would allow the council to propose legislation without his permission.

Attacks continued in 2004, many of them linked to al Qaeda. A car bomb at the security forces' headquarters in Riyadh killed four and wounded 148 in April of that year. The following month, an attack at a petrochemical site in Yanbu killed five, while an attack and hostage taking at an oil company compound in Khobar claimed 22 lives. Three gun attacks in Riyadh within a single week in June caused the deaths of two Americans and a BBC cameraman. That same week an American engineer was kidnapped and beheaded, his filmed death later released. At the end of that year, an attack on the U.S. consulate in Jeddah killed five staff members.

The Saudi family did respond to these potentially dangerous events. From February to April 2005, nationwide municipal elections were held in Saudi Arabia, the first since the 1920s. Women did not participate in this tentative step toward democracy.

On August 1, 2005, King Fahd died. He had been ill and hospitalized for two months before his death. The kingdom quickly announced that his half brother Abdullah would succeed him. Abdullah had served not only as crown prince but also as head of the national guard, which managed Saudi Arabia's internal security. While King Fahd had been clearly pro-American, Abdullah was less eager to cement ties with the West.

The rise of Abdullah to the throne renewed focus on the system of succession that had served Saudi Arabia since the death of Abdul Aziz Ibn Saud in 1953. Abdullah was believed to be 82 when he became king. At what point would the sons of Ibn Saud no longer rule the kingdom he had created? And what would be the impact when a new generation assumed the throne?

Abdullah's half brother, 81-year-old Prince Sultan, was named the new crown prince. Sultan had served as Saudi Arabia's defense minister, and his son Bandar represented Saudi Arabia as ambassador to the United States for two decades. He also had had health issues in the past, including treatment for a cancerous growth in his stomach in 2004.

When Abdullah took over as king, he faced numerous challenges, including his kingdom's security, with militants increasingly calling for an end to the presence of any Westerners in the kingdom and the replacement of the monarchy by an Islamic regime. Meeting the demands of increasingly restive citizens required him to take concrete steps to address the issues of unemployment, oil pricing, and calls for modernization and an end to corruption within the royal family.

## A LOOK AHEAD

In many ways Saudi Arabia is caught in a strange kind of isolation—an isolation that permits only a few features of modernity but otherwise remains little changed from the kingdom built by Abdul Aziz. The number of schools and universities in the kingdom has increased, and television and the Internet have brought foreign influence. In the holy city of Mecca, pilgrims now find Starbucks, Tiffany, and H&M. There is a shopping mall with fast-food restaurants and an amusement-park ride.

The municipal elections of 2005, which were heralded as a sign of democratic progress produced local councils that were largely ineffective. They passed resolutions that were nonbinding, with little or no impact on the Saudi government's plans. Increasingly, the government has begun to crack down on those calling for political change. Women remain marginalized, forbidden from doing things that women in many other countries take for granted, such as driving cars.

Addressing concerns about the succession to the Saudi throne, and to prevent serious infighting among the next generation of princes, King Abdullah changed the constitution so that the senior members of the royal family would elect a crown prince from a group of candidates selected by the next king. He also moved away from the once-firm alliance with the United States, labeling the American presence in Iraq (beginning with military operations in 2003) "an illegal foreign occupation."

To the surprise of many who forecast its demise decades earlier, the Saudi monarchy survived the twentieth century. But much has changed since Abdul Aziz unified Saudi Arabia in

Almost 2 million Muslims from all over the world gather in Mecca, Saudi Arabia, once a year in order to fulfill one of the five pillars of Islam, the hajj. *Above*, pilgrims gather at a fast food restaurant offering special meals near the Grand Mosque during the hajj in 2001.

1932; the kingdom has been marked by great contradictions and even greater challenges.

The country that holds approximately one-fourth of the world's proven oil reserves has become a political force in the Middle East and the world. But its population is growing quickly, far outdistancing the ability of even the most progressive regime to provide employment opportunities.

The increasing number of young people, many of them well educated but with few job prospects, has spread discontent through the streets of Riyadh and other Saudi cities. This trend encourages the growth of political extremism, and there has been great concern in recent years about the swift spread of more radical Islamic elements in Saudi Arabia, preaching an anti-Western, anti-monarchist philosophy. The increasing influence of the ulama has contributed to the imbalance by training more clerics at Islamic universities—few of whom can find jobs in mosques—and by stressing religious instruction in schools rather than the technical skills that can secure a job in the twenty-first century. Saudi Arabia has also spread Wahhabism throughout much of the Islamic world by funding religious schools that preach a doctrine of intolerance toward non-Muslims.

The challenges—both to the Saudi-U.S. relationship and to the royal family—will persist well into the twenty-first century. Saudis care about resolving the Israeli-Palestinian conflict. Additional concerns focus on the perceived threat posed by Iran, by instability in Iraq, and what role Saudi Arabia should play in the region.

The politics of modern Saudi Arabia have largely been based on three focal points: Islam, security, and oil. As the modern Middle East took shape around it, the kingdom remained true to its position as guardian of the holy cities of Mecca and Medina, while enjoying the economic benefits of oil and the security it could provide. But in the twenty-first century, these three points are sometimes at odds with one another. The politics that bring security and the wealth that oil provides conflict with the more austere framework of the Wahhabi faith.

The empire that Abdul Aziz shaped is now an economic power, and his sons have become some of the wealthiest men in the world. The past is still clearly visible in Saudi Arabia. But the future of the kingdom is far from certain. Five times a day, around the world, devout Muslims turn toward Saudi Arabia, toward the city of Mecca, in prayer. The direction in which Saudi Arabia turns in response to the challenges of the twenty-first century will be of critical importance not only to the kingdom but also to the faith its leaders have sworn to protect.

# Chronology

| | |
|---|---|
| 1902 | Abdul Aziz (Ibn Saud) conquers Riyadh. |
| 1914 | Sykes-Picot Agreement signed. |
| 1921 | Cairo meeting held; Middle East divided and rulers appointed. |
| 1924 | Mecca conquered by Saudi army. |
| 1932 | Kingdoms of Najd and Hijaz unified and Kingdom of Saudi Arabia created. |
| 1938 | Oil discovered at Dammam Dome. |
| 1953 | Death of Abdul Aziz. |
| 1960 | OPEC is formed. |
| 1964 | King Saud abdicates; Faisal becomes king. |
| 1973 | King Faisal launches oil embargo against United States. |
| 1975 | King Faisal assassinated; Khalid becomes king. |

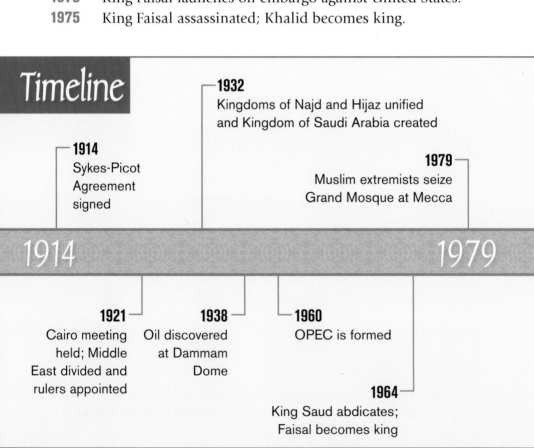

## Timeline

**1932**
Kingdoms of Najd and Hijaz unified and Kingdom of Saudi Arabia created

**1914**
Sykes-Picot Agreement signed

**1979**
Muslim extremists seize Grand Mosque at Mecca

1914

1979

**1921**
Cairo meeting held; Middle East divided and rulers appointed

**1938**
Oil discovered at Dammam Dome

**1960**
OPEC is formed

**1964**
King Saud abdicates; Faisal becomes king

1979    Muslim extremists seize Grand Mosque
        at Mecca.
1982    King Khalid dies; Fahd becomes king.
1990    Saddam Hussein invades Kuwait and threatens
        Saudi Arabia.
1991    Gulf War begins.
1995    King Fahd suffers stroke; Crown Prince Abdullah
        assumes management of kingdom.
2001    Al Qaeda launches attacks against New York City and
        Washington, D.C., on September 11; 15 of the 19
        hijackers are Saudi nationals.
2003    United States announces that it will pull out almost
        all of its troops from Saudi Arabia.
2005    Nationwide municipal elections are held; King Fahd
        dies on August 1 and is succeeded by his half brother
        Abdullah.

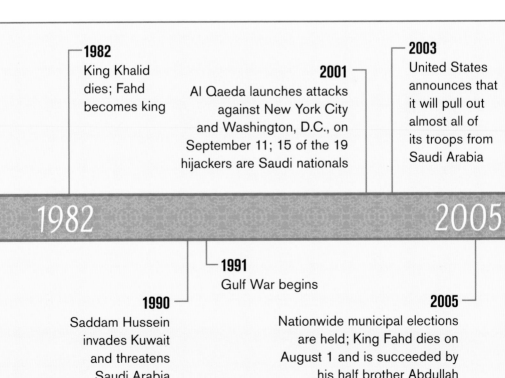

**1982**
King Khalid dies; Fahd becomes king

**2001**
Al Qaeda launches attacks against New York City and Washington, D.C., on September 11; 15 of the 19 hijackers are Saudi nationals

**2003**
United States announces that it will pull out almost all of its troops from Saudi Arabia

1982                                          2005

**1991**
Gulf War begins

**1990**
Saddam Hussein invades Kuwait and threatens Saudi Arabia

**2005**
Nationwide municipal elections are held; King Fahd dies on August 1 and is succeeded by his half brother Abdullah

2006    King Abdullah formalizes succession system for future kings.

2007    Kingdom responds to concerns about behavior of religious police with new restrictions on the detaining of suspects; royal decree orders a review and overhaul of the judicial system.

# Bibliography

Abir, Mordechai. *Saudi Arabia in the Oil Era*: *Regime and Elites, Conflict and Collaboration.* Boulder, CO: Westview Press, 1988.

Al-Farsy, Fouad. *Modernity and Tradition: The Saudi Equation.* New York: Kegan Paul International, 1990.

Bradley, John R. *Saudi Arabia Exposed: Inside a Kingdom in Crisis.* New York: Palgrave Macmillan, 2005.

Champion, Daryl. *The Paradoxical Kingdom: Saudi Arabia and the Momentum of Reform.* New York: Columbia University Press, 2003.

Doughty, Charles M. *Travels in Arabia Deserta.* New York: The Heritage Press, 1953.

Fattah, Hassan M. "After Saudis' First Steps, Efforts for Reform Stall." *New York Times*, April 26, 2007, *http://www.nytimes.com/2007/04/26/world/middleeast/26saudi.html?partner=rssnyt&emc=rss.*

———."The Price of Progress: Transforming Islam's Holiest Site." *New York Times*, March 8, 2007, *http://www.nytimes.com/2007/03/08/world/middleeast/08mecca.html?pagewanted=1.*

Howarth, David. *The Desert King*: *A Life of Ibn Saud.* New York: McGraw Hill, 1964.

Jehl, Douglas. "A Nation Challenged: Saudi Arabia; Holy War Lured Saudis as Rulers Looked Away." *New York Times*, December 27, 2001, *http://query.nytimes.com/gst/fullpage.html?res=9A01E0DD1031F934A15751C1A9679C8B63&sec=&spon=&pagewanted=all.*

Johnston, David. "Two Years Later: 9/11 Tactics; Official Says Qaeda Recruited Saudi Hijackers to Strain Ties." *New York Times*, September 9, 2003, *http://query.nytimes.com/gst/fullpagehtml?res=9803E4DD143BF93AA3575AC0A9659C8B63.*

Lacey, Robert. *The Kingdom.* New York: Harcourt Brace Jovanovich, 1981.

Mackey, Sandra. *The Saudis.* Boston: Houghton Mifflin, 1987.

Randal, Jonathan. *Osama: The Making of a Terrorist.* New York: Alfred A. Knopf, 2004.

Shadid, Anthony. "Abdullah Becomes Saudi King on Death of Half Brother Fahd." *Washington Post*, August 2, 2005, p. A1.

Slackman, Michael. "Cultural Collisions in the Slow Lane to Modernity." *New York Times*, May 9, 2007, *http://www.nytimes. com/2007/05/09/world/middleeast/09saudi.html*.

Stewart, Desmond. *T.E. Lawrence*. New York: Harper & Row, 1977.

Wallach, Janet. *Desert Queen: The Extraordinary Life of Gertrude Bell: Adventurer, Adviser to Kings, Ally of Lawrence of Arabia*. New York: Anchor Books, 1996.

Wilson, Jeremy. *Lawrence of Arabia*. New York: Atheneum, 1990.

## Web sites

www.arabnews.com

www.bbc.co.uk

www.nytimes.com

www.washingtonpost.com

# Further Resources

Al-Rasheed, Madawi. *A History of Saudi Arabia*. New York: Cambridge University Press, 2002.

Bradley, John R. *Saudi Arabia Exposed: Inside a Kingdom in Crisis*. New York: Palgrave Macmillan, 2005.

Howarth, David. *The Desert King*. New York: McGraw Hill, 1964.

Lacey, Robert. *The Kingdom*. New York: Harcourt Brace Jovanovich, 1981.

Mackey, Sandra. *The Saudis*. Boston: Houghton Mifflin, 1987.

Vassiliev, Alexei. *The History of Saudi Arabia*. New York: New York University Press, 2000.

## Web sites

**Arab News-The Middle East's leading English language daily newspaper**

www.arabnews.com

**BBC Country Profile: Saudi Arabia**

http://news.bbc.co.uk/2/hi/middle_east/country_profiles/791936.stm

**The New York Times: Times Topics Saudi Arabia**

http://query.nytimes.com/beta/search/query?query=saudi+arabia&srchst=cse

**The Royal Embassy of Saudi Arabia in Washington, D.C.**

http://www.saudiembassy.net/Country/Country.asp www.spa.gov.sa

**The Washington Post: Country Guide Saudi Arabia**

www.washingtonpost.com

# Picture Credits

**Page:**

8  Infobase Publishing

12  AP Images, Rahimullah Yousafzai

17  AFP/Getty Images

21  Infobase Publishing

24  Corbis

28  © Bettmann/Corbis

33  AP Images, Amr Mabil

37  Time & Life Pictures/Getty Images

44  Courtesy of the Library of Congress, [matpc 12206]

47  © Reuters/Corbis

50  Infobase Publishing

56  Getty Images

61  AP Images, Hasan Sarbakhshian

66  Getty Images

71  AP Images

74  AFP/Getty Images

79  Getty Images

82  AFP/Getty Images

84  AFP/Getty Images

87  AFP/Getty Images

91  Infobase Publishing

93  AP Images, U.S. Navy

97  AFP/Getty Images

# Index

## A

Abdul Aziz ibn Saud
    death, 68, 95
    family honor, 27, 29, 31–32, 68
    fight for power, 30–32, 34, 54
    followers, 31–32, 45, 60
    monarchy of, 10, 34, 35–55,
       57–59, 62, 68, 70, 73, 97,
       99
Abdullah
    government, 65, 85, 88,
       94–97
Abdullah bin Ali, 47–48, 51
Afghanistan, 14
    invasions of, 11
    military, 11, 15
al-Haram, 59
Al-Hasa
    control of, 40–41, 63
al Qaeda network
    force, 11–13, 15
    leader of, 9, 11, 13
    militants, 94
    terrorist acts of, 7, 9
    training, 14
al-Rashid family
    end of, 48–49, 51
    military of, 30–31, 36, 38–39,
       41, 48
    overthrow of, 32
    reign of, 27, 29–32, 37
Anayzah, 38
Anwar Sadat, 80, 85
Arabia
    control of, 54–55, 59
    lands of, 22, 26–27, 29, 35,
       38–40, 43, 45, 47, 51
Arabs
    community, 19
    forces, 11, 16, 22–23
    lands, 19, 52, 80, 82, 85
    language and customs, 19, 23
    nationalist movement, 78–80,
       82, 85
    people, 38, 70, 72
    promises of unity and
       independence, 18, 24, 40,
       70–71, 75
    revolt, 22–25, 42, 45, 55, 87

## B

Bahrain, 52, 63
Bedouins, 27
    army of, 29, 38
    customs, 62
    leaders, 32, 34–36, 42–43, 46
Begin, Menachem, 85
Beirut, 18
bin Laden, Muhammad, 9
    construction company, 10–11,
       13
    death, 10
bin Laden, Osama
    acts of terror, 9, 11, 14–15
    allies and enemies, 13–15
    birth, 10
    childhood, 9–11
    citizenship, 13
    education, 11
    family, 9, 11–13
    fortune, 11
    marriages, 11, 13
    military, 11–12, 14–15, 93
Bosnia, 15

## C

Camp David Accords, 85
Carter, Jimmy, 85
Chechnya, 15
Cheney, Richard, 13

Churchill, Winston, 49
Cox, Percy, 37–38, 42, 51
Crane, Charles R., 62

**D**
Damman Dome, 65
Dhahran, 94

**E**
Eastern and General Syndicate, 52
economy, Saudi Arabia
    oil, 7, 26, 51–52, 62–66, 69–74, 80–82, 92, 99
    pilgrimages, 45
    problems with, 62
    reforms, 78, 98
Egypt, 19, 49, 55
    government, 70, 72–73, 80
    military, 76, 81–82
    peace treaty with Israel, 85
Eisenhower, Dwight, 72
Empty Quarter, 26–27, 31

**F**
Fahd ibn Abdul Aziz
    reign, 83, 85, 87–88, 94–95
Faisal bin Hussein, 23–25
    and the Arab revolt, 42, 49, 60, 65
Faisal Ibn Abdul Aziz
    assassination, 82–83
    reign, 68–70, 72–82
Faisal Ibn Musaed, 82
France, 51, 72

**G**
George V, King of England, 16
Germany
    government, 19, 30, 41, 65
    military, 20
Golan Heights, 81
government, Saudi Arabia
    constitution, 97
    corruption, 69, 72

Council of Ministers, 70, 72, 75
    foreign policy, 42
    monarchy, 7, 10–11, 13–15, 85, 97
    plan of succession, 64–65, 73, 83
    reforms, 76, 97
    spending, 73
Great Britain
    financial support from, 54–55
    government, 16, 18–20, 25, 37–38, 40–43, 45–47, 49, 51–52, 54–55, 57–58, 63, 65, 70, 72
    intelligence services, 19–20, 54
    military, 16, 23, 30, 41
    society, 19
    trade, 42

**H**
Hijaz, 32, 43, 49
    attacks on, 54–55, 57, 59
    control of, 62
    unification, 60
Hogarth, David, 19
Holmes, Frank
    oil projects, 51–52, 62
Hussein bin Ali
    government, 43, 45–47, 49, 51–55
    instability, 54–55, 57–60
    military, 54

**I**
India, 25, 55, 57
Iran, 20
    government, 85
    and oil, 75
    at war, 90, 92
Iraq, 45
    borders, 49
    control of, 54–55, 60, 63

government, 12–13, 20, 90
military, 13, 89–92
and oil, 75
at war, 90, 92
Islam
causes, 69
declaration of faith, 60
extremists, 14–15, 94, 96
forces, 11, 14, 20
Hadith, 46
Ikhwan, 46, 48, 54, 58, 60, 86
Koran, 35, 46, 86
law, 88
tenets of, 79
Wahhabi branch, 7, 15, 34–35, 45–46, 57–58, 68–69, 83, 87
Israel, 72, 76
government, 80–81
military, 81
peace treaty with Egypt, 85
Italy, 65

J
Japan, 81
Jeddah, 9–10, 43, 59
Jerusalem, 10, 76
Jewish people
homeland, 66–67, 80
Jordan (Transjordan), 55, 80
Juhayman ibn Muhammad ibn Sayf al Utaybi, 85

K
Kennedy, John F., 76
Kenya, 14
Khalid ibn Abdul Aziz
reign, 83, 85, 87–88
Kosovo, 15
Kurmah, 48
Kuwait, 63
government, 29–30, 38, 40, 82, 90
invasions of, 13, 30

military, 31, 89–90
oil in, 29, 63, 75
ports of, 30, 34
at war, 90, 92
wealth in, 27, 29

L
Lawrence, T.E. "Lawrence of Arabia"
controversy, 18, 25
expert on the Middle East, 18–20, 22–25, 42–43, 49
humble beginnings, 18–19
illness, 18
and the military, 16, 18, 22–23, 25
Lebanon, 49, 54

M
Masjid al-Haram, 10, 85
Masjid al-Nabawi, 10
Mecca, 9
conquest of, 57–59
control of, 26, 32, 35, 39, 43, 45, 47–48, 98
mosques in, 10, 55, 88
pilgrimages, 33, 43, 45, 53–55, 58–59, 69
sharif of, 42–43, 45, 54–55
Medina, 10
control of, 26, 32, 35, 39, 43, 45, 57, 59, 98
mosques in, 55
Middle East, 11
influence to, 19, 49
information about, 16, 18–20
modern, 15
partitioning of, 63
rulers, 62, 68
turbulence in, 7, 66
military, Saudi Arabia, 86
battles for expansion, 58
early battles, 31–36, 38–41, 47–49

Mubarak al-Sabah
   military, 30
   rule of Kuwait, 29–30, 34,
      38, 40
Muhammad
   teachings, 35, 46, 55, 58, 60
Muhammad ibn Abd al-Wahhab,
   35
Muslims
   community, 57, 92
   holy cities, 26, 53, 86, 98
   mosques, 10, 59, 86
   Shiite, 85
   traditions, 27, 32–33, 35, 39,
      43, 45, 53, 57–58, 69, 86
   unity, 79
Mustafa Kemal Atatürk, 55

N
Najd
   unification, 60
Nasser, Gamal Abdel,
   Egyptian leader, 70, 72–73, 76
   nationalism, 78, 82
Nazareth, 18

O
Onassis, Aristotle, 69, 71
OPEC. See Organization of the
   Petroleum Exporting Countries
Operation Desert Storm, 92
Organization of the Petroleum
   Exporting Countries (OPEC),
   75, 81
Ottoman Turks
   caliphate, 55
   corruption, 22–23
   destruction of, 20, 22–23, 40
   government, 26–27, 30, 32,
      41–43, 45, 70
   land, 16, 18, 20, 22, 49
   military, 20, 22–23, 37–39, 42
   success and growth of, 20, 26

P
Pakistan, 13
Palestine, 18–19, 45
   borders, 49
   control of, 54–55
   invasions, 23
   Jewish homeland in, 66–67,
      85
people, Saudi Arabia, 7, 73
   classes, 11
   population, 14
   programs, 69
   rebellions, 56
   social reform, 94
   and terrorism, 9
   and women's rights, 78
   youth, 14
Persian Gulf, 32, 37, 40, 65
Philby, Harry St. John, 63
Powell, Colin, 94
public education, 78

Q
Qatif, 51

R
Red Sea, 9, 45
Riyadh, 10
   attacks on, 27, 29, 48, 93–95
   liberation of, 76
   recapture of, 30–32
   reign of, 26, 34–36, 42, 45–
      48, 53, 59, 68
Roosevelt, Franklin, 67
Russia, 80

S
Saddam Hussein, 12–13, 90
Saud family
   history of, 26–27, 29, 35,
      37–39, 42
   honor, 27, 31–32, 68
   leader of, 34

Saudi Arabia
    borders, 13, 26, 48, 76
    foreign policy, 85
    future, 97–98
    history of, 26–39
    modernization, 60, 68, 86,
        97
    relationship with United
        States, 7, 13–14, 52, 64, 72,
        80, 92, 98
    today, 20
Saud Ibn Abdul Aziz
    corruption, 69
    reign of, 64, 68–77
September 11, 2001, terrorist
    attacks
    events of, 7, 9, 14–15
Shakespear, William, 40–42
Sinai Desert, 22
Six-Day War, 80
Socal. See Standard Oil Company
of California
Soviet Union, 72
    military, 11
Standard Oil Company of
    California (Socal), 63–65
Standard Oil of New Jersey, 73
Sudan, 13
    government, 14
Suez Canal, 23, 67, 72, 81
Sultan bin Abdulaziz al-Saud, 13
Syria
    borders, 49
    control of, 54
    government, 80–81
    invasion, 23
    lands of, 10–11, 18–20, 45,
        49, 51

T
Taif, 10, 57–58
Taliban
    government, 14–15

Tanzania, 14
terrorism
    attacks, 7, 9, 14, 93–94
    training camps, 14
Thompson, Campbell, 19
Transjordan. See Jordan
Tripoli, 18
Truman, Harry S., 67
Turkey, 18, 40
    government, 55
Twitchell, Karl, 62–63

U
United Airlines Flight 93, 7, 9
United States
    government, 13–14
    military, 13–15, 72, 76, 80,
        92–94
    oil companies, 62–66, 69,
        71–73, 81–82
    relationship with Saudi
        Arabia, 7, 13–14, 52, 64,
        67, 72, 80, 92, 98
    terrorist attacks against, 7, 93

V
Venezuela
    and oil, 75
Vietnam, 80

W
Wilson, Woodrow, 62
Woolley, Leonard, 19
World Trade Center, 7, 9
World War I
    aftermath, 25, 43, 46–47
    events of, 16, 19, 22–24, 41–
        42, 63, 65

Y
Yemen, 9, 14, 76
    trainees, 11–12
Yom Kippur, 81

# About the Contributors

Author **Heather Lehr Wagner** is a writer and editor. She earned a B.A. in political science from Duke University and an M.A. in government from the College of William and Mary. She is the author of more than 40 books for teenagers on global and family issues. She is also the author of new editions of *Iran*, *Iraq*, and *Turkey* in the CREATION OF THE MODERN MIDDLE EAST series.

Series editor **Arthur Goldschmidt Jr.** is a retired professor of Middle East History at Penn State University. He has a B.A. in economics from Colby College and his M.A. and Ph.D. degrees from Harvard University in history and Middle Eastern Studies. He is the author of *A Concise History of the Middle East*, which has gone through eight editions, and many books, chapters, and articles about Egypt and other Middle Eastern countries. His most recent publication is *A Brief History of Egypt*, published by Facts On File in 2008. He lives in State College, Pennsylvania, with his wife, Louise. They have two grown sons.